TRADING WITH AMERICA

S0-DYR-970

This book is dedicated to my wife Pamela
and our three children, Rachel, Ashley and Jennifer,
who patiently sacrificed many evenings and weekends while
I worked on this book,
and to my parents who made it all possible.

David N Kay

Thanks are also due from me to my wife Isabel,
who suffered months of untidiness and
displayed her usual patience during the book's preparation.

Ernest Kay

Trading with America

David N Kay
Ernest Kay

Gower

© David N Kay and Ernest Kay 1997

All rights reserved. No part of this publication may be reproduced, stored in a retrieval system, or transmitted in any form or by any means, electronic, mechanical, photocopying, recording or otherwise without the permission of the publisher.

Published by
Gower Publishing Limited
Gower House
Croft Road
Aldershot
Hampshire GU11 3HR
England

Gower
Old Post Road
Brookfield
Vermont 05036
USA

David N Kay and Ernest Kay have asserted their right under the Copyright, Designs and Patents Act 1988 to be identified as the authors of this work.

British Library Cataloguing in Publication Data
Kay, David N.
   Trading with America
   1. Great Britain – Commerce – United States   2. United States – Commerce – Great Britain
   I. Title II. Kay, Ernest
   382'.0941'073

ISBN 0 566 07685 3

Phototypeset in 11/13pt Palatino by Intype London Ltd.
Printed in Great Britain by Biddles Ltd, Guildford.

Contents

Preface

The purpose of this book is to identify some of the issues which frequently arise when trading with America. However, it does not replace the need for professional advice from a lawyer, accountant or business adviser before signing on the dotted line. This is particularly the case with respect to the checklists and sample agreements in the Appendices. These should be used as a guideline for negotiations only; they should not be regarded as a definitive 'standard form' agreement, as each agreement must reflect the business arrangement and understanding between the parties.

The authors would like to thank those who have provided material which has been incorporated into this book, especially material available through the DTI.

This is the first of what is intended to be a number of editions of this book. To make the book more useful to those involved in the process of trading with America the authors would welcome any comments or suggestions which can be incorporated into future editions.

David N Kay
Ernest Kay

1 Introduction

This book is written for those organizations that are contemplating trading in one way or another with the United States of America. It treats the subject seriously and where necessary in depth, and at the same time, in areas of fringe interest, provides guidance for those who wish to consult source material on specific points.

Many businesses, whether sole proprietorships or small or large corporate entities, are looking to broaden their markets territorially. Interested readers could range from the entrepreneur who is selling a product into the American market, to the business executive negotiating a merger with, or acquisition of, a US company.

Following the recent spate of activity in exports from one European country to another, which was encouraged by the removal of the various inhibiting barriers such as tariffs, taxes and duties, many companies are now directing their attention to markets further afield. Not surprisingly, this attention is being directed towards what is currently the world's largest single market, the United States of America.

Regional differences

Many of those trading with or considering trading with the USA, whether by direct or indirect selling or by licensing, encounter difficulties arising from various sources, such as cultural, social, legal and financial. Not least is the realization of the sheer size of the territory and the fact that although America is frequently regarded as one market-place, this is not the case. From Texas to Alaska, from Maine to California, there are some 50 states, each with differing climates, politics, legal systems and usually different market demands. For example, a product with high demand in Texas could have a low or virtually zero demand in Minnesota.

In Chapter 2 these differences are considered with reference to commercial exploitation. Before attempting to trade with the USA, it is necessary to have some knowledge and understanding of the most important of these differences. It surprises many to find that language features in them. Spanish is frequently heard in the south-western regions, particularly in California and New Mexico.

UK sources of information

Anyone intending to trade with the USA must consider how and where information relevant to markets and market demand can be obtained and the sources of factual material relevant to marketing outlets in each region.

A great deal of information concerning markets and marketing exists in the UK, together with a wealth of advice on factors such as cultural and legal which enable the entire concept of selling into the USA to be put into perspective. The UK Department of Trade and Industry, various chambers of commerce and the US embassy would be the first points of enquiry. The sources of material relevant to a particular technical field and intended territorial area, as available in the UK, are discussed in Chapter 3, and the more important contact addresses are given in Appendix 9.

US sources of information

Chapter 3 also deals with the many sources of information which are available in the USA on a regional basis. UK businesses are advised to make an initial evaluation using material available from European sources before seeking further help from the USA. In this way, specific regions of interest can be targeted. The cost of obtaining information from US sources to cover the entire country can be very considerable, not to mention time-consuming, and it is much more economical – in terms of both time and money – to obtain preliminary information from the 'home' source. Once your initial plan for market penetration has been formulated, further detail can be obtained from US sources, including the various British–American chambers of commerce, the embassy and other trade bodies. Access America, a trade advisory organization, can provide comprehensive marketing information with useful background material for specific selected areas.

Protect your rights

Having dealt with the preliminaries of marketing and related surveys, the next step is to consider what you intend to make available to the American market and how well you are protected should any attempt be made to copy your product or use your information. If your material, be it product or process, is commercially interesting, you may be sure that your competitors, present or future, will take a long and careful look at it with a view to assessing your competitive edge and will consider modifying their own product or strategies in order to remain competitive or develop alternative forms for commercial exploitation.

Intellectual property

Before entering into discussion with third parties and perhaps providing samples, you should have the protection of intellectual property rights. These rights include patents, trade marks, designs and copyright, and extend into trade secrets and know-how, together with means of disclosure protected by a confidentiality agreement, thereby providing a safe means of exploitation by, for example, licensing.

The whole subject of intellectual property (otherwise known as 'industrial property') is one of rapidly increasing importance, and the laws concerning it vary considerably throughout the world. One factor which must be borne in mind is that the protection (registration) of your intellectual property in the UK does not necessarily mean that it is protected in the USA.

Many of the problems and conflicts encountered when establishing markets in the USA arise because of a lack of understanding of the legal rights attaching to a product or process. Establishing and registering your legal rights and then incorporating them in your subsequent activities, by contract and agreement, is of paramount importance.

What are these legal rights? Chapter 4 explains and takes you through the rather awesome concept of intellectual property and, within its fringe, the commercial aspects of intellectual property – licensing and franchising. Together with agency and distributorship agreements, these form the means of commercial exploitation of intellectual property.

Insure your rights

Having taken all the necessary steps to ensure that your products and processes have been protected in both the UK and the USA, by the filing of patent applications, the registration of trade and service marks, the correct designation of (and perhaps lodging of) copyright and the signing of a confidentiality (non-disclosure) agreement, your next step would logically seem to be one of exploitation – to convert your expenditure in the USA into a positive cash return. In order to sell your product in the USA or to license your process involves talking to other parties, showing your product, perhaps permitting trials, disclosing your method of manufacture and planned improvements and future developments. You may have chosen an agent to represent you or a distributor to handle your goods, or, if you are intending to permit another company to manufacture using your process, a licensee or joint venture partner. Whatever route you choose, you must make disclosures of a technical, financial or marketing nature to a party you have known for perhaps only hours.

Before opening discussions or entering into negotiations with a third party one factor must be considered. Although disclosure may be made under secrecy, any agreement to maintain confidentiality can be breached, your product or process can be copied, your trade mark/name used without your permission. As soon as you make disclosures to third parties, even though you have filed patents or protected your ideas in other appropriate ways, you are at risk. Any breach of agreements, copying of ideas or products whether it be actual or merely suspected, if they are to be effectively checked and stopped could incur expensive litigation. It is not unusual for the costs encountered in a case of unfair competition or patent infringement to exceed £300,000 in Europe and be well in excess of $700,000 in the USA.

In the case of product liability matters (discussed in Chapter 5), the cost including the payment of any damages awarded can be over $1 million, and you as manufacturer or merely seller could be involved in an action in the event that your product resulted in harm to a user.

Types of insurance

Fortunately, insurance is available to minimize your cost of involvement in these court actions, and these matters are covered in Chapter 6. Insurance against personal liability and general litigation costs resulting from breach of contract have been available for some time, but it is only recently that insurance can be taken out in respect of costs for the legal enforcement or defence of intellectual property rights, costs and damages in respect of product liability claims and costs incurred by the licensor or licensee for action against contract breach. This insurance is not only available for the UK and mainland Europe but extends internationally and includes the USA to a limit of indemnity corresponding to the higher costs of litigation in that country and the not infrequent award of higher levels of damages.

In order to avoid pitfalls you should take out this type of insurance at an early stage in your discussions. You could find the name you intend to use infringes a US trade mark (such a trade mark may not exist in the UK) or copyright used only in the USA. In addition, you may find that the use of your product in a demonstration or trial results in damage or harm.

Prudent commercial awareness indicates that you must protect yourself against claims and ensure you are financially able to enforce your rights. According to the Advisory Council on Science and Technology, 'Intellectual property which cannot be defended through the courts is property without value.' As you will see later, the cost of this type of insurance is only a small proportion of the cost you incur when obtaining intellectual property rights internationally, of selling your product in the USA or of setting up a manufacturing base by self-manufacture or by licence.

Liability for your product

Closely linked with the general topic of insurance is that of product liability. In the USA the notion of strict liability applies. Although we have seen that insurance is available to reduce the economic consequences of a lawsuit, such a claim can have far-reaching commercial consequences; the adverse publicity alone could seriously affect your business. It is therefore better to consider how the risk of product liability claims can be minimized rather than by merely relying upon insurance cover.

Chapter 5 considers the US view of product liability and the various methods available to minimize the risk. The US principles of product liability relate to the special liability of the seller of a product for physical harm to the user or consumer.

Anyone who sells any product in a defective condition and which is unreasonably dangerous to the user or consumer or to his property is subject to liability for any physical harm which it causes to the ultimate user or consumer or to his property. The law applies even if the seller has exercised all possible care in the preparation and sale of his product. In other words, liability is strict and is an attempt to shift the burden of accidental injury from the one who is injured to the manufacturer or seller.

Managing the risk

But the risk can be managed, and there are numerous ways in which manufacturers in particular can establish certain safeguards to reduce their exposure. Chapter 5 sets out the more important of these 'preventative management' ideas, including anticipating product use, or abuse, giving adequate instructions and warnings if the product is inherently hazardous and issuing disclaimers and warranties.

Exploiting your ideas, solely or jointly

You should by now have carried out any necessary market research and studies associated with introducing your product or process to the USA. Those of your trading tools and innovative ideas which can be considered as intellectual property rights have been legally protected to avoid copying, and where this is not possible, or, as additional protection, the appropriate non-disclosure agreements have been signed. To further protect, you will have taken up the most appropriate of the insurance options available.

You are now ready to commence practical exploitation in the USA. You may decide to introduce your product by direct selling, perhaps using the various warehousing, stockholding and dispatch facilities which exist in various regions of the USA.

Some of these are operated by UK companies. Alternatively, you may appoint an agent who will work on your behalf to locate suitable licensees if you have a process to license, or suitable marketing outlets or partner if you have a product to sell. You may consider teaming up with an established distributor in those states in which you wish to introduce your product. The agent would be able to locate suitable distributors for you, or you may find them yourself by using information from the Department of Trade and Industry and other organizations.

In the case of certain products associated with a service-type arrangement, you may feel that franchising could be a desirable route. This involves the screening and appointment of suitable franchisees and involves much the same principles as that of the licensor–licensee relationship.

A more complex working arrangement for exploitation would be a joint venture, which is considered in Chapter 7, where the operation and effects of this type of working arrangement are reviewed.

Trading sole, partnership or corporate

Although a further decision must be made at the initial stages on whether to trade as a sole proprietor, a partnership, a corporation or as a limited liability company, many commence trading in the USA on the same legal basis as in the UK. The various legal forms corresponding to the various methods of trading that have been discussed are considered in Chapter 7. The flexibility of the status of sole proprietor and of partnership must be contrasted with corporate or limited liability status with its less flexible operation.

The correctly chosen legal entity for trading can greatly affect the future success and smooth operation in the years ahead. If you already exist as a UK company you may be inclined to set up a trading office in the USA as a US subsidiary. Alternatively, if you are operating in the UK as a sole trader or as a partnership, you may wish to project the same image in the USA, at least during the early phases of introduction. The personal disadvantages of doing so are emphasized.

Publicity and advertising

Having decided upon your trading status, the next step must be to present your product and/or process to those who would buy it or form some kind of trading relationship with you to sell or to manufacture the product. Various methods and media for advertising and achieving publicity are considered in Chapter 8.

It is an important pre-selling activity to inform the public and alert potential buyers to the fact that the product is available to them, setting out what the product does and its advantages over those of your competitors. You can do this by various means, the principal ones being:

- Advertising
- Trade fairs and exhibitions
- Publicity in various magazines, trade periodicals and on television.

Chapter 8 also includes information concerning the more important regular trade fairs and exhibitions in the USA to help you to introduce your products, and attention is drawn to the various trade fair directories currently available.

Routes for exploitation

For many products that are already established in the UK and mainland Europe, there are various methods available to achieve commercialization in the USA and these are considered in Chapter 9. Direct export selling appeals to many UK exporters, though heavy involvement and commitment of both time and money is required, especially if you set up your own US office. But the whole process of commercialization can be made much easier if you use a distributor, or you have a manufacturer's representative or selling agent in those states you have selected as your first entry points. The role of the various companies which assist with exporting is an interesting one: Chapter 9 shows that certain of these have headquarters in the UK but have a warehouse and distribution network in the USA, which provides a relatively easy way for you to establish yourself in the US market without the need for a physical presence.

For manufacturing and service companies without well-established selling facilities, licensing and franchising can be the least costly route of getting your product on to the shelves of the retail outlets. The overall financial returns are generally less, but granting a licence rather than 'going it alone' can be the difference between success and failure.

Transportation services

You must consider carefully the means of transporting your goods to the USA. The methods of doing this are considered in the same Chapter 9 together with a review of the required documentation. The shipper requires various invoices and packing notes, with certificate of origin and accompanying banking documents, shipping note, bill of lading and export customs entry. The services of a freight forwarder, linked with those of a customs house broker, make the day-to-day operation of exporting and importation run more smoothly. The problems associated with US customs and effecting entry of your goods can be solved by using a US importer who will clear the goods through customs, pay the necessary duties and deal with transport to the destination.

Other related matters such as classification of goods, tariffs and the effect of international trading agreements such as GATT (administered by the World Trade Organization) and NAFTA are considered in this chapter.

Finance

In all trading matters it is continually necessary to consider aspects of finance. Profitable and efficient management is the key to success, and finance must be looked at in an international context, taking into account currency fluctuations and foreign exchange risks, as well as different trading laws and customs. The use of the internationally accepted documentary credit/ letter of credit is reviewed in Chapter 10 as one of the most effective means of receiving payment for your goods.

The importance of bank involvement in matters of the general operation of export credit and financing, money transfer and letters of credit are all discussed in relation to the commercial operation, together with a consideration of the US tax systems in relation to trading. As with all countries, US tax laws are different from those of the UK and those differences which affect your trading are highlighted.

Staffing

An increasing level of staffing involvement will inevitably follow successful entry into the US market, and the recruitment and employment of staff may follow hard on the heels of your preliminary approaches in America.

The many important issues to be addressed on the question of recruitment and employment are handled in Chapter 11.

Employment laws

The equal employment opportunity laws at both state and federal level, as well as affirmative action regulations, have a significant impact on the way each employer recruits and hires personnel. Procedures must be free from any implication of discrimination. We give an in-depth consideration of pre-employment issues and review the employment policy in relation to both non-union employees with their 'employment at will' doctrine and union employees who are protected by federal legislation.

As your trading activity gains momentum you may need to transfer some of your UK-based staff to the USA and one of the issues connected with the establishment of a retail outlet or manufacturing unit in the USA is that of entry requirements for non-citizen staff. Chapter 11 deals with US immigration law and its impact on foreign-owned businesses.

Visas

Any person who is not a citizen of the USA must obtain a non-immigrant (temporary) or immigrant (permanent) visa status by the US government in order to be permitted to enter and/or remain in the country for any period of time.

Understanding the relationship between and consequences of US tax and corporate laws on the one hand and US immigration law on the other is crucial to minimizing US or foreign tax liability. The various types of visas are discussed in Chapter 11, which will enable anyone establishing business to understand which is required and how it can most effectively be obtained.

Federal laws

Chapter 12 deals with certain federal laws, that is, those laws which apply throughout the USA as opposed to state and local laws which apply only in a specific state or defined locality, respectively.

The USA is a very litigious nation (it has more lawyers than all other countries of the world combined). In fact, Americans do not hesitate to commence legal proceedings against others, and you must bear this in mind when signing agreements, contracts or other documents with legal consequential effects. You must seek professional legal guidance before signing, and the earlier in your process of negotiation that you have this advice, the fewer will be the problems that arise.

With that caution, the important federal laws considered in this 'legal chapter' relate to anti-trust issues, securities and environmental issues.

Laws relating to employment, product safety and quality, advertising and selling, and banking and finance are discussed in earlier chapters.

Anti-trust issues

The USA has one of the oldest and strictest anti-trust (cartel) laws in the world. Unlike the anti-trust laws of the European Community, American law provides for jail terms of up to three years and criminal fines for a narrow range of 'hard core' offences such as price-fixing and market sharing, and also makes provision for private 'treble' damages suits.

US anti-trust law is based on three main statutes. The first is the Sherman Act, which prohibits unreasonable restraints of competition between competitors and those in the chain of distribution. It also prohibits monopolization, attempts to monopolize and conspiracies to monopolize. The second is the Clayton Act, which supplements the Sherman Act and prohibits anti-competitive acquisitions and mergers. The third is the Robinson–Patman Act, which prohibits certain forms of price discrimination.

These statutes are enforced by the Anti-Trust Division of the Department of Justice, the Federal Trade Commission and by private parties.

These anti-trust laws have a strong bearing on virtually all aspects of trading including distribution restraints, resale price maintenance, price-policing policies and cutting of discount reselling as well as acquisition, joint venture, patents and licensing and, of course, price discrimination.

Securities laws

Also of considerable bearing on your trading are the securities laws. These include the Federal Securities Act of 1933 and the Securities Exchange Act of 1934. These Acts regulate the issuance or sale of securities to the public, securities being defined broadly to include stocks, bonds, options, certain partnership agreements and other investment contracts.

In addition, most states regulate issuance and exchange of securities in their respective jurisdictions using the 'Blue Sky' laws, which may apply even if the exchange is exempted under federal security laws. It is important that companies seeking to do business in the USA as a corporation realize that federal and state securities laws may apply to both the initial issuance and any subsequent transfer of company stock.

Environmental issues

Few doing business in America will not feel the impact of the environmental laws. These are also dealt with in Chapter 12, and include the following five primary enactments relating to:

(*a*) the requirement that federal agencies address environmental concerns when reviewing public projects they fund or when approving or funding private projects: the Environmental Policy Act (EPA);

(*b*) the regulation of the management of hazardous waste from its inception to ultimate disposal: the Resource Conservation and Recovery Act (RCRA);

(*c*) the regulation of the pollution of the air above threshold quantities by stationary sources – for example, factories, and by mobile sources, such as motor vehicles: the Clean Air Act (CAA);

(*d*) the setting of concentration limits for water pollutants in water bodies: the Federal Water Pollution Control Act, otherwise known as the Clean Water Act;

(*e*) the imposition of liability for the remediation of sites where hazardous waste was disposed of in the past: the Comprehensive Environmental Response, Compensation and Liability Act (CERCLA).

The CERCLA imposes very tough liability for hazardous waste sites not only as created by current owners and operators but also on previous owners and operators of the site.

Resolution of disputes

No book on trading would be complete without dealing with the subject of dispute resolution. Doing business with and investing in another country creates a need for contractual arrangements to be set up and agreements to control these arrangements. The various means of dealing with and resolving the disputes which arise when the contractual relationship breaks down are dealt with in Chapter 13.

Although there are a substantial number of lawsuits each year in America, relatively few proceed to resolution by the courts. Many are resolved through arbitration, and provision is frequently made for this in contracts and agreements. For the international-type agreements where the two parties are from different countries, the advantages of arbitration over conventional courtroom litigation include savings in time and expense, confidentiality of the proceedings, expertise of the arbitrators, neutrality (the domestic courts can be avoided) and ease of enforcement.

But to go to arbitration or to settle differences in court should always be a last resort. Negotiation for the settlement of disputes, that is, mediation by the two parties or involving outside mediators, is to be recommended. The initiation of legal or arbitration proceedings for the settlement of a dispute frequently causes irreparable damage to the relationship between the parties. Mediation, however, can avoid this breakdown, leading to a mutually acceptable solution to the dispute and allowing the trading relationship to continue.

Appendices

The Appendices provide practical help in your task of setting up your export business. Guidance is given in respect of some of the basic agreements you will require to negotiate and have prepared. The checklist of contents of a distributorship and a licence agreement are set out in Appendices 1 and 2 respectively, so that you know what information to provide to your lawyers when you have such agreements prepared. The text of a typical distributorship and licence agreement is set out in Appendices 3 and 4 respectively.

An example of a confidentiality and non-disclosure agreement is set out in Appendix 5.

Appendix 6 sets out the information required for one of the trade documents – the bill of lading – with which you will frequently come in contact so that you are aware, in advance, of the material you will need to provide to complete this document.

Appendix 7 sets out the information required for one of the most important and most frequently encountered financial documents – the letter of credit.

Appendix 8 contains a summary list of commodities useful for product identification when importing into the USA.

Appendix 9 sets out a list indicating certain organizations and institutions with addresses and telephone numbers that will provide advice and help to those actively trading or merely contemplating trading with the USA.

Appendix 10 is a glossary of many of the more commonly encountered commercial terms.

Appendix 11 sets out some of the more important arbitration clauses used in agreements.

Appendix 12 is a list of useful publications.

Appendix 13 lists certain British–American Chambers of Commerce with addresses and telephone numbers in various areas of the USA.

Graphic overview

Finally, as a check-list for your operation Figure 1.1 sets out a general overview of the contents of the book as it deals with the various matters relating to the selling route – from conception of invention through to retailing or exploiting by licence. Needless to say, for those proceeding to manufacture by licence or with

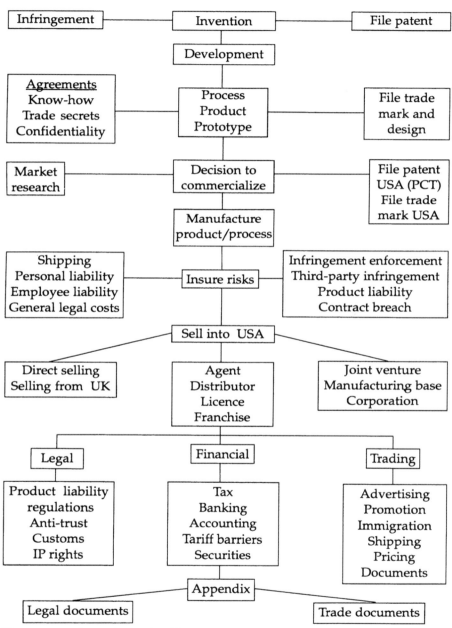

Figure 1.1 Overview of selling route

a product already well established in their own territory, certain steps set out in this schematic overview will have already been taken.

2 The United States of America

The sheer enormity of the USA often deters many potentially successful exporters from trading with that country. But what do most business people understand by the term 'United States of America' and its distinction from what is frequently referred to as 'North America' and the similar term 'The Americas'?

Quite simply, the Americas means the entire continental boundaries of the northern and southern areas from Canada and north Alaska down to the southernmost tip of Argentina. North America is often used when referring to the northern part of 'The Americas', that is, the United States of America and Canada. The United States of America is that area of North America which excludes Canada. Including Hawaii and Alaska, the United States of America is made up of 50 states. In addition, the USA has external territories including Puerto Rico and the US Virgin Islands.

The map at Figure 2.1 shows the location and relative sizes of the regions. The USA is the fourth largest country in the world, having an area of some 9.4 million square kilometres and extending some 4500 kilometres from east coast to west coast and some 2570 kilometres from north to south. In all, the

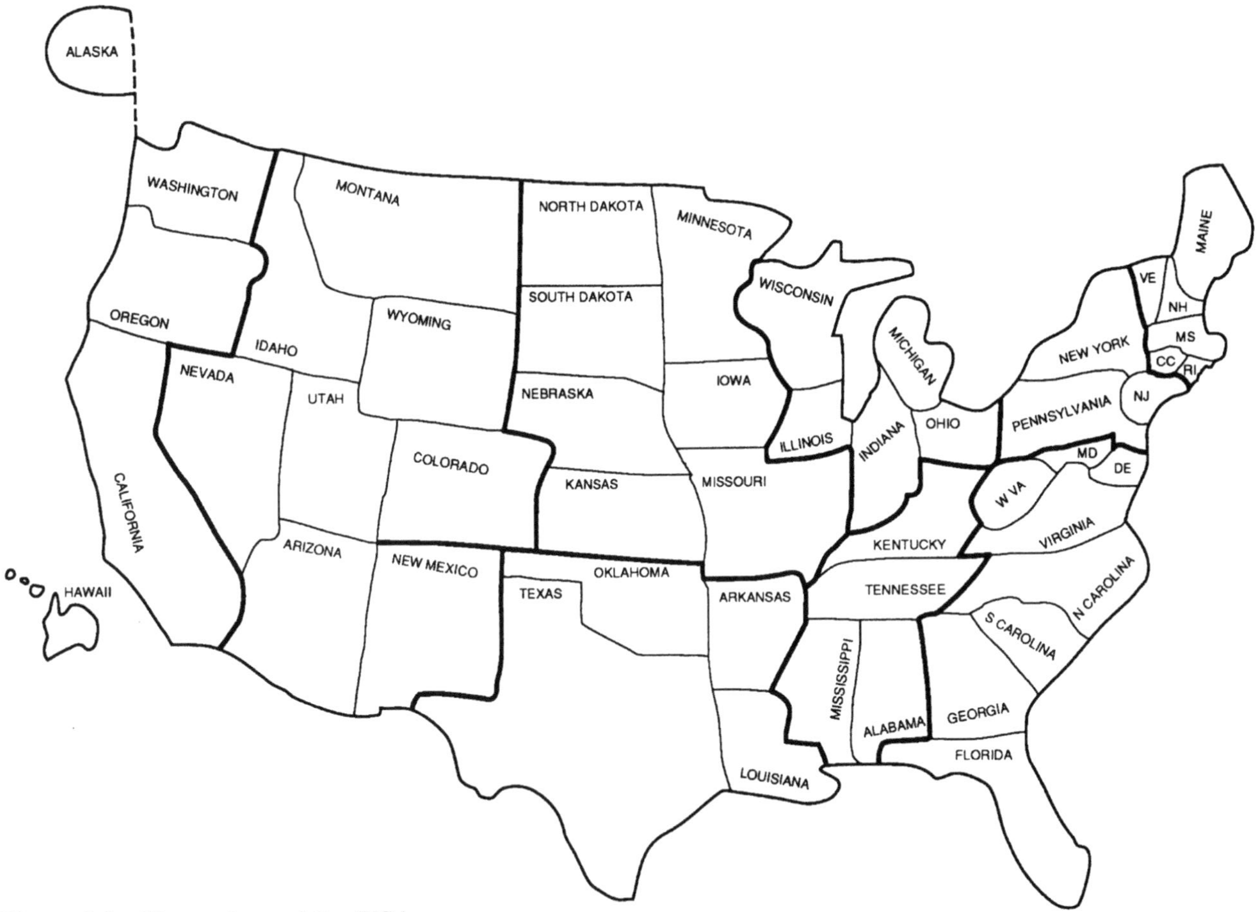

Figure 2.1   The regions of the USA

USA is more than twice the combined size of the European Union and has a population of more than 250 million – more than the population of the European Union.

Of most importance commercially is the fact that the USA is the largest importer of goods and services and is one of the most industrialized countries in the world.

Although, in size, the USA is vast, if you divide it into regions, then into individual states, the concept of establishing a market there becomes more manageable. For example, you could select the East North Central region, and focus on Illinois and Michigan for the initial importing initiative. Here, you will find Chicago and Detroit, the former a dynamic city with more than eight million people – population-wise, third only to New York and Los Angeles. It is located at the southern tip of Lake Michigan and is a major terminal for road, rail and air transport, being regarded as the point for transport where east meets west. It is a centre of enormous manufacturing and food processing activity and has a greater variety of industries than any other state. Chicago's O'Hare International Airport is said to be the busiest in the world and is a central US hub for both domestic and international air lines. Illinois is also one of the leading states in finance, commerce and culture.

Detroit, lying 280 miles north-east of Chicago at the confluence of Lakes Huron and Erie, has a population of about five million and has the largest single-industry labour force of any city. It is also the largest consumer of raw materials and partially manufactured goods. The automobile manufacturing centre is located in Detroit.

Together, the area forms a good jumping-off ground in the USA, imported goods having easy access by sea, rail and air. It is also worthy of note that the British–American Chamber of Commerce is very active in the area and gives importees every advice and help available.

Having dispelled some of your misgivings associated with size, it is a useful next step to look at some of the factors which influence any decision concerning selling into the USA.

The first to look at is the *climate* of the country. This varies greatly across the country. In the north-west, Alaska has a temperature below zero for much of the year, while Hawaii and Florida in the west and south respectively vary from tropical to warm temperatures all the year. There are also great differences in temperature from east to west. Seasonal variations on the east coast are similar to those experienced in the UK, while on the west coast, in California, temperature variations between summer and winter are much less noticeable, the temperature remaining consistently high. It is in the East North Central areas, or mid-west, where extremes of temperature ranges between summer and winter are most pronounced – variations from 33 °C in summer to −15 °C in winter are the norm.

It is these regional and seasonal variations which must be studied very carefully when you are making plans to introduce your product into the USA. There is no point in attempting to introduce and sell swimwear in Alaska as the market would be extremely small compared with Florida all the year round, or Illinois in the spring and summer.

Another factor which affects market planning and product introduction is that of *language*. In all regions of the USA, English is the generally used and official language, but there are areas, for example, Chicago, New York and the south-west, running down to Mexico, where there is a substantial Polish-, Italian- and Spanish-speaking population, respectively.

There is also a considerable Asian population in the west and the north-east, and this must be taken into consideration in overall plans for marketing or product introduction.

In much the same way, *education* and the differences of achievement between regions are important factors. Most children in the USA attend school until the age of 16 but in some states the school-leaving age is 18. The educational system generally is divided into primary and secondary levels, with college and university education available to those who have obtained a secondary-school graduation certificate. Some 13.5 million Americans attend, at any one time, one of the 3000 colleges or universities in their country. Of the many students receiving a first or bachelor's degree (around one million each year and increasing), almost a third go on to further education to obtain a master's or doctor's degree.

Something must be said of the other factors affecting product introduction, although in some instances to a relatively small degree.

Political   Politically, the USA is a federal republic consisting of 50 states. The capital city is Washington in the District of Columbia (not to be confused with the State of Washington on the west coast).

The federal government comprises three divisions:

(a)   Congress – the legislative body made up of the Senate and the House of Representatives, the latter being made up of Democratic and Republican parties.

(b)   Civil service – the executive branch, headed by the president, which is responsible for law enforcement and the control of foreign affairs. The various heads of executive departments make up the cabinet, an advisory body to the president.

(c)   Judiciary – a branch of the government consisting of a system of courts of which the final court of appeal is the Supreme Court.

Separate from the federal government are the governmental bodies of each state. Each state has its own governor with powers divided between executive, legislative and judicial affairs. It is important to appreciate that each state has the right to enact and enforce its own laws.

The demographic and social structure of the US population   In any market into which new products are to be introduced, it is prudent to consider the various territorial areas of the USA and the demographic and social status and trends of each territorial area.

It is generally accepted that the economic and social changes taking place in the USA at present will lead to an era of economic growth and a considerable increase in living standards. The fluctuations in birth rate over the past 60 years has resulted in a situation where the growth in the number of people in the

35–55 age group, when family income and spending are at its highest, is growing rapidly. This group is expected to grow by as much as 25 per cent in the next ten years. One figure of staggering significance is that, of the entire increase in consumer spending in the USA, 80 per cent is expected to be due to the 35–55 age population.

This factor, coupled with the growth in the number of American working women, will profoundly influence marketing decisions when new products and new territories are being considered. There is a great deal of statistical information relevant to trading available, and a summary of the more important information on territory, population, spending capacity and social make-up differences across the USA is given in Figure 2.2. It must be stressed that the figures have been given for comparative purposes only and are to be used solely as an indication of relative trends. Before you make use of this information the material must be verified, as statistical change frequently takes place.

Because the USA covers such a large area, extending over some 3.5 million square miles, the US government has divided the country for statistical purposes into nine areas. These areas are followed closely by the DTI in its literature and are shown in Figure 2.1. The regions covered are:

1   New England – Maine, New Hampshire, Vermont, Massa-chusetts, Rhode Island, Connecticut.
2   Middle Atlantic – New York, New Jersey, Pennsylvania.
3   East North Central – Ohio, Indiana, Illinois, Michigan, Wisconsin.
4   West North Central – Minnesota, Iowa, Missouri, North Dakota, South Dakota, Nebraska, Kansas.
5   South Atlantic – Delaware, Maryland, District of Columbia, Virginia, West Virginia, North Carolina, South Carolina, Georgia, Florida.
6   East South Central – Kentucky, Tennessee, Alabama, Mississippi.
7   West South Central – Arkansas, Louisiana, Oklahoma, Texas.

Figure 2.2 Economic indicators for the US regions

	New England	Middle Atlantic	South Atlantic	East North Central	East South Central	West North Central	West South Central	Mountain	Pacific
Relative size	1.8%	2.8%	7.5%	7%	5%	15%	12%	23.9%	25%
Population	5%	15%	18%	17%	7%	7.5%	10.5%	5%	15%
Major states	Rhode Island Massachusetts Connecticut Maine Vermont New Hampshire	New York New Jersey Pennsylvania	Maryland Virginia West Virginia N/S Carolina Georgia Delaware Florida DC	Ohio Indiana Illinois Michigan Wisconsin	Tennessee Alabama Mississippi Kentucky	Minnesota Iowa Missouri North and South Dakota Nebraska Kansas	Louisiana Oklahoma Texas Arkansas	Colorado New Mexico Arizona Nevada Montana Idaho Wyoming	California Oregon Washington Alaska Hawaii
Major Cities	Boston (33% [of region's population] Hartford	New York (50% of region's population) Philadelphia Pittsburgh	Washington-Baltimore (15%) Miami (7%) Atlanta (7%)	Chicago (19%) Detroit (11%) Cleveland (7%)	Memphis Jackson Louisville	St Louis Minneapolis-St. Paul Des Moines	Dallas (16%) Houston (14%) New Orleans (5%)	Phoenix Denver (together more than 30%)	Los Angeles (35%) San Francisco (17%) Seattle (7%)
E — Total US personal income	6%	16%	17%	17%	5-0%	7%	9-5%	5-5%	17%
C / O / N — Average Household Earnings	$42,000	$40,000	$37,000	$37,000	$30,000	$37,000	$33,000	$36,000	$42,000
O / M — Households earning >50,000	33%	30%	25%	25%	17%	25%	22%	25%	30%
Y — Wives Working	33%	56%	60%	60%	50%	66%	60%	60%	60%
Household heads with degree	33%	25%	30%	25%	20%	25%	25%	30%	33%
Commerce	Culture Finance Insurance Intellectual centre (Harvard, Yale and Princeton)	NY leader in finance, culture, commerce	Federal government in Washington DC Finance Banking	Chicago 2nd leader in finance, commerce and culture	Finance Insurance	Commerce Manufacturing Company headquarters	Financial centre in Dallas	Hi-tech Corporate offices	Finance Insurance Aeronautical
Industry	No mass production, small specialist, e.g. computers, electronics.	Steel, shipping, aircraft. Active industries of many kinds. NY major port and major industrial centre	Light and some heavy industry Textiles, food processing	Light and heavy chemical and engineering. Automobile. Chicago leader in industrial activity Food processing	Some light industry Greenfield sites	Mining and refining of ores Food processing	Oil and petroleum Chemical industry	Mining and refining of minerals Tourism and skiing	Hi-tech manufacturing Film and video, aircraft, aerospace and missiles, automobile, clothing
Agriculture	Some dairy, fishing, timber	Moderate farming area	Fruit, seafood	Meat, grain, timber, dairy	Cotton, tobacco, soy beans	Corn, dairy, timber	Cotton, livestock, general farming	Cattle, sheep	Fish, vegetables, timber
Future trends	Slower growth than average	Slower growth than average	Faster growth than average	Slower growth than average	Slower growth than average	Slower growth than average	Moderate growth	Faster than average growth	Substantial growth in both population and income

8   Mountain – Montana, Idaho, Wyoming, Colorado, New Mexico, Arizona, Utah, Nevada.
9   Pacific – Washington, Oregon, California, Alaska, Hawaii.

In conclusion, it can be said that the rapidly changing social and economic forces at work in the USA are resulting in an accelerating development of consumer interest and demand. New markets are continually opening up, and existing markets are being developed in such a way that smaller and more specialized areas and demands must be satisfied.

It is the company or business with the ability to spot these trends and developments, and react to satisfy them and exploit the opportunities, that will benefit most. Being first will frequently help in exploitation, but this may not be sufficient. The quality must be high, follow-up service and guarantee must be excellent, and the price must be competitive.

The next chapter will help to indicate the sources of information needed to evaluate the markets and spot the trends and opportunities.

3 Market Research

Selling a new product to consumers requires a certain amount of market research. This applies whether you sell into domestic markets or sell abroad, but nowhere is it more important than if you intend to import and sell into the USA.

You must ascertain the present state of the market and evaluate this in relation to the targets you have set. In this way, you reduce the business risk which must inevitably attach to your venture. If you know the overall market size and market trends in respect of potential customers, the activities of your competitors, the prices charged for similar products and, perhaps most of all, the niche in the market which your product can fill, you will have much of the basic information you need to reach the commercial decision as to whether to export to the USA and, if so, how and where (and perhaps when).

Information on all products and market trends is available and is relatively easy to obtain. The USA has a tendency to document all facts which could be needed in the future – the main problem is for you to find them. What you want to know will be available somewhere, but where and how will you find it?

This chapter deals briefly with the main sources available in the UK and the USA. Addresses are set out in Appendix 9.

It is not necessary to deal with general works giving information on market research because you will already be aware of them, though the more familiar ones are set out in Appendix 12. In researching the US market there are three important factors to bear in mind:

- the size of the country;
- the cost of the market research;
- the time-span within which you need the information.

It is therefore necessary to attempt initially to concentrate your efforts in certain regions. Industry is concentrated in certain centres: for example, gas and oil in Texas, aerospace on the west coast, automobiles in Detroit and a broad spread of general industry in Chicago (see Figure 2.2). Similarly, population is clustered and concentrated in certain areas, such as Chicago and Detroit, New York and Los Angeles. In Chicago and Detroit alone you will find a vast market of more than 13 million eople, many of whom are earning well above the nation's average.

Let us briefly set out those sources of US marketing information which are readily available in the UK at reasonable cost.

The first step should be to contact the DTI regional offices, and local offices connected with the DTI, for example Business Link, the addresses and telephone numbers of which, and some names, are set out in Appendix 9. You should arrange an initial meeting, which is free of charge, and set out your predetermined needs and criteria. The DTI can help on many issues and in many areas. Unfortunately, it is such a vast organization that it may take time and effort to reach the person who is best able to help – you must have patience and perseverance. The facilities available to you at low cost will give you invaluable information and will help with your assessment of the markets. According to their own literature, as supported by many exporters, the DTI can:

- give advice as to the information you need in your first stages leading to export;
- suggest general reading materials;
- advise on the availability of material in reference and other libraries;
- put you in touch with others who have experience of establishing themselves in US markets;
- introduce you to the Export Marketing Information Centre of the DTI in London;
- provide access to on-line databases;
- provide an introduction to the US desk of the DTI in London which will give advice and provide information and may suggest contact with consular staff in specific regions of the USA.

The diplomatic staff can often either gather together the information or point the way to suitable sources. For example, the British diplomatic staff in the USA could make an information-gathering study for the entire country for as little as around £300. A charge for further time will be made at the rate around £130 for eight hours, and this information can be very detailed for specific regions. Check the up-to-date cost of their services before going ahead.

Sources of information
Local reference libraries are usually well stocked with reference material on exporting to the USA and frequently carry basic directories such as *Thomas's*. They can also direct you to business libraries, often at colleges and universities, and will effect the necessary introductions for a personal search. But often the business librarian will give you a considerable amount of personal help: it is usually well worth your while to ask!

Export Marketing Information Centre, London.   This centre, with free access, is well equipped with trade directories, market research reports, statistical surveys of all kinds, mail-order catalogues and US governmental publications, and provides access to many US databases. Although some find it difficult to use for the first time, the staff are able to provide help and will guide you through the maze of material. Provided you have a clear objective and know what you want to export and sell and have some idea of the preferred regions, the Centre will either be able to turn up the information you require, or will direct you farther to the more specialized sources.

It is in the Centre where you will find many of the more important source materials. A list of the more frequently used publications follows, but other sources are given in Appendix 12.

US Industrial Outlook
Forbes Annual Report on American Inventory
Census of manufacturers (US Department of Commerce)
Detailed demographic surveys (Bureau of Census)
Statistical Abstract of the USA – very useful for ascertaining
    population and marketing trends
Dun & Bradstreet, *Million Dollar Directory*
Standard & Poor's *Register of Corporations, Directors and*
    Executives
Moody's *Industrial Manual*
Predicasts Basebook
Predicasts Forecasts
Index of Articles Published (Predicasts)
MacRae's Blue Book – listing products and companies
Thomas's Register – index of companies in 12 volumes
MacRae's lists of manufacturers' representatives
Cahners Product Directory
Cahners Address Directory
Ward's Directories – 51,000 largest US corporations and 49,000
    largest private US companies
Sheldon's Retail Directory
Trade Names Directory
Encyclopedia of Associations – lists trade associations in the USA
    – invaluable for making contact with the most appropriate
    US trade associations
National Directory of Addresses and Telephone Numbers
Forbes 500 – largest US companies

Municipal yearbooks
Industrial Directory of Published Market Research
Trade associations
US government
Databases
DTI, which publishes reports on US markets – a list of these
   is available from DTI Export Publications.
Chambers of commerce and industry

Additional sources of information are available in the USA and can be accessed during a personal visit. During such a visit you will be able to have discussions with those involved in your areas of interest – distributors, retailers, customers – on a face-to-face basis or by telephone.

As a result of your market research work you will have targeted relevant organizations and associations and, by forward planning from your UK base, meetings can be arranged for information gathering. This aspect of forward planning cannot be stressed too much. So many have travelled to the US for information gathering and for meetings only to experience the frustration and disappointment, particularly in the first few days of the visit, of non-availability of those you planned to meet.

However, although we all know that it is most important to do some kind of market investigation before entering the market, for many the time involved is too great. The alternative is to use a consultant to do some or all of the work for you. Talk to the DTI and someone in the British Commercial Office in that part of the USA where you are intending to do your market research.

Very helpful sources of information are the various British–American chambers of commerce or business associations throughout the USA. These chambers and associations can assist foreign companies doing business in their regions. Their databases and membership resources can also assist in 'match-making' UK companies with their US industrial counterparts. Many of these chambers of commerce and business associations have a UK membership category which enables British companies to join for a nominal fee and thereby obtain information, newsletters, business briefings and the like on the region.

The New York British–American Chamber of Commerce has offices in London, the North American Business Club has offices in Bristol and the British–American Business Group in the North West has offices in Cheshire. The addresses and contact information for each of the chambers and business organizations are listed in Appendix 13.

The British–American Business Council also plays a very active role in the development of trade and UK/US business relations. The Business Council consists of all the British–American business associations and chambers of commerce throughout the USA and the UK, and its aim is to enhance trade and investment between the two countries and to provide information, products and services to members. The Business Council has appointed an International Advisory Board consisting of the chairmen and chief executives of leading British and American corporations as well as the ambassadors of both the US and UK governments.

It is advisable to meet some of the consultants recommended to you before making your final choices, and essential to get a cost estimate for the work they will do.

4 Intellectual Property

Intellectual property defined

The term 'intellectual property' is relatively modern. It was formerly known as 'industrial property' – a term which conjured up the concept of factories and warehouses, but not what was intended.

The modern 'intellectual property' term captures the concept of the creation of intellect – inventions, ideas, special names, designs, works of art – and are defined and protected as the legal rights of patents, trade marks, designs and copyright.

Also falling under this broad umbrella is the commercially valuable material encompassed by the concept of trade secrets and know-how, protected by the familiar confidentiality or non-disclosure agreement.

A further extension of intellectual property covers the means by which patents, trade marks and copyright can be commercially exploited. This is by licensing, franchising and through agency and distributorship arrangements. These latter are considered elsewhere.

Let us first consider one of the most important of the intellectual property rights, the patent.

Patents

Definition and scope of the patent right

Patents protect processes, machines, articles of manufacture and compositions of matter that are new, not obvious and useful. Patent protection is available only through the grant of a patent. A patent gives the inventor the right to prevent others from making, using or selling the invention for a period of time. This is 20 years from the date of application in the UK, and 17 years from the date of issue or 20 years from the date of filing in the USA. The patent grant confers on the inventor a monopoly right to have exclusionary commercial enjoyment (making, using, selling and licensing to others) in the country of grant for the term of the patent in exchange for the disclosure to the public of the invention as set out in the patent specification. This patent right is only exclusionary, not exclusive – in other words, it is a negative right only. Thus, a patent owner has no affirmative right to use the invention if making, using or selling it would infringe another's valid patent.

Infringement

The unauthorized manufacture, use or sale of a patented invention is an infringement of that patent right if the process or product falls within the scope of the statement of the claim of the patent. It may also be an infringement to supply and assemble parts of the patented invention. The patent owner can take court action against an infringer, and if successful can be awarded damages and/or an injunction against the infringer to stop the infringing act. In the USA damages may be trebled if the infringement is wilful or the case otherwise exceptional, and under these circumstances attorneys' fees may also be awarded.

Of course, it is not necessary to patent your invention, and you may decide to keep secret the process of manufacture or the crucial step in the process or vital ingredient in the formulation and exploit alone or with others, using as protection for your trade secrets and know-how a confidentiality and non-disclosure agreement. This route has much against it, principally that secrecy cannot always be maintained and breach of the confidentiality and non-disclosure agreement can be difficult to prove.

Patent protection in the UK

Having made the decision to protect your process or invention by patent, you will first file your patent application in the UK patent office. You should use a qualified patent agent, although the Patent Office provides numerous good information booklets on patents and patenting. The UK system enables a patent application to be filed in a basic, incomplete form with only informal drawings at a lower cost than that of a full application. It allows a subsequent 12-month 'breathing space' during which time the application must be completed by the filing of an amplified description with fuller details of how the process is carried out or a better description of the product and a set of claims, abstract and formal drawings, with a request for an official search of the published material in the same technical field as your invention.

Patent protection in the USA

During this 12-month 'breathing space' you must file in the USA so that the first filing date (priority date) will be given to the filing in the USA as accorded under the international convention on patents. You can either file a patent application directly in the USA, or file a worldwide patent application, known as a PCT (Patent Co-operation Treaty) patent application. This latter route is a means of filing a patent application virtually worldwide through the World Intellectual Property Organization in Geneva and having the facility to select certain countries in which to proceed, at a later date, to seek patent grant.

US and UK patents compared

Having filed the full application in the UK, the traditional procedure is that six months later the contents will be published and details of your invention will then be available to the public.

The application will pass through various stages of examination at the Patent Office and, if accepted, the patent will be granted not later than four and a half years after first filing. The procedure in the USA is different in certain respects, particularly in that the contents of a US patent application are kept confidential during the entire application process. (It is expected, however, that this will change and the availability will then follow European practice.) Publication in the USA occurs only when the patent issues. Even the fact that you have filed a patent application is kept secret, there being no disclosure of the name of the applicant or the title of the invention as occurs in the UK at the time of filing.

This confidentiality has the advantage that the owner of an invention is not obliged at an early stage to make a choice between filing a patent or keeping a trade secret. While applying for a patent the invention can be protected as a trade secret, and that protection will remain even if the patent application is rejected.

Unlike most other countries, such as the UK, where a patent cannot be obtained if a disclosure or commercialization of the invention occurs before the first filing date (priority date), in the USA an applicant has a one year 'grace period' after its public disclosure or commercialization to file for a patent.

Trade marks

Definition and rights
A trade mark is a word, name, symbol or device (or any combination of them) used by a manufacture or trader to identify his goods and distinguish them from the goods of others. A service mark differs from a trade mark in that a service mark identifies the source of services, rather than the source of goods. Rights in a mark in the USA are acquired by actually using the mark on or in connection with goods or services. Rights may also be reserved by filing an application for federal registration of the mark, and this would be the means of obtaining a registered

mark corresponding to the mark already registered in the UK. These rights are enforceable in the USA (unlike the UK) only if the mark is continually used afterwards. Trade mark rights in the USA continue indefinitely as long as a mark is used and renewal fees paid.

UK practice

While there is no legal requirement to register a trade mark in the UK, it is advisable to do so as registration offers exclusionary rights to the mark for the goods or services concerned. Furthermore, if a mark is unregistered and its use is insufficient to acquire a reputation in the market (and therefore cannot be defended in a passing-off action) the owner would not have prior rights against a later-registered mark. Should you decide not to seek registration of a mark, or if your application to register is unsuccessful, your trade mark can still be used as an unregistered mark.

Effect of registration in the USA

In the USA, unlike many other countries, trade mark rights are acquired through use of the mark, without the need to register it. None the less, registration of a trade mark in the Patent and Trade Mark Office plays an important role in protecting trade mark rights. Registration is initial evidence of trade mark ownership, and is a prerequisite for recording the mark with the US Customs Service to prevent the importation of infringing foreign goods. The most significant benefit of federal registration is incontestability; use of a registered mark is more difficult to challenge once the mark has been registered and used continuously for five years. Generally, in the USA, before a mark can be registered, goods bearing the mark must be shipped in interstate or foreign commerce. Foreign trade marks are exempt from this requirement if the mark is registered, or registration has been applied for, during the preceding six months in the country of origin.

Because a trade mark can be registered in the USA irrespective of the status of the mark in the UK, we shall deal solely with the process of effecting trade mark registration in the USA.

US practice

Obtaining a trade mark registration in the USA typically takes over a year. A written application, specimens of the mark and a statutory filing fee are filed with the Patent and Trade Mark Office. The registration is issued only after the Patent and Trade Mark Office has performed a search to ensure that the mark will not cause confusion with previously registered marks and is otherwise entitled to registration. Even if the application is approved, interested parties may initiate an administrative opposition proceeding to prevent registration of the mark.

Maintaining your mark

To maintain the registration once it has been issued, the registered mark must be used. Token use is no longer sufficient. A declaration of use must be filed during the sixth year after registration, and continued use must be confirmed when the registration is renewed every ten years. Non-use of a mark for two consecutive years is ordinarily considered abandonment, and the registration may then be cancelled.

Infringement

The owner of a trade mark can maintain an infringement action against anyone whose use of the same or a similar mark may cause confusion. Courts typically issue an injunction against future infringement, and may award monetary damages. If the infringement is wilful, the court may award treble damages and attorneys' fees.

Protecting your mark

When you are using your trade mark you ought to mark the goods, packaging, advertising and all related material with an indication that the mark is a trade mark. You can, for example, use ® if the mark is registered or the symbol ™ if it is not registered. It is also important not to use the mark as the name of the goods or services but to use the mark as an adjective in conjunction with the appropriate generic name for the goods or services. This ensures that the trade mark is always associated with yourself as the trader and does not become the generic name for goods or services, regardless of origin.

Copyright

Definition and scope

A copyright is an exclusive right granted by US federal law to the creator of an 'original work of authorship' to reproduce, display or perform his work. Typical 'works of authorship' include books, music, films, sculpture and photographs. Even technical or business-oriented works, including computer programs, are protectable under copyright.

In order that works can be protected as copyright they must be original, but the requirement for originality has a low threshold: the work must be the author's own creation and must be more than a 'trivial variation' on an existing work.

Copyright protects the expression of an idea and not the idea itself, though an idea of a commercially useful nature could fall within the realm of patents. Mere facts in isolation are not capable of benefiting from copyright, but a compilation of such facts may be protected by copyright if such a compilation conforms with the minimum level of creativity and originality required by US law.

Copyright term in the USA

A work enjoys federal copyright protection from the moment it is created and fixed in a tangible form, whether or not it is later published. The copyright lasts for the creator's lifetime plus 50 years after his or her death, unless the creator is anonymous or his life span is not known, when the term of the copyright is 75 years. Although the copyright notice requirement has now been abolished, use of the notice is still recommended as a deterrent to infringement and for the procedural advantages that it provides in the event of infringement. Furthermore, the infringer cannot claim he was an innocent infringer if the copyright symbol and details are displayed. The copyright notice consists of (i) the symbol ©, or the word 'copyright', (ii) the year of first publication, and (iii) the name of the copyright owner.

Registration in the USA
To register, you must deposit two copies of the work, an application and a fixed fee with the Copyright Office in Washington DC. Although the Copyright Office examines the work to ensure that it is a 'work of authorship' entitled to protection under copyright, no effort or searching is undertaken to determine originality. It is important to appreciate that registration of your copyright in the Washington DC office has the effect of making your material open to public inspection once it has been lodged. This is quite different from patent and trade mark registration.

Infringement
A copyright generally is infringed by the unauthorized reproduction of the work. Unauthorized importation also constitutes infringement, even if the imported copy was lawfully made abroad. Federal law makes wilful copyright infringement for profit a crime. Civil remedies in the form of an injunction against future infringement and monetary damages (including attorneys' fees) are available.

The USA, along with most other major industrialized countries, is a party to the Berne Convention, an international treaty on copyright protection. This means that the published work by a national of most major industrial countries will automatically be protected in each of the other member countries.

UK law
In the UK the law governing copyright is the Copyright, Designs and Patents Act 1988 which makes provision for a new form of protection, the unregistered design right. The act transfers protection of engineering drawings to prevent the manufacture and sale of the functional article depicted in the drawings from the realm of copyright to that of the unregistered design right. As there are no such provisions in the USA for unregistered design rights we shall not concern ourselves with such protection.

Commercial secrets and know-how

Almost without exception, any commercial business has ideas and information which relate to the technical and general business operation, which are valuable and which are not known to outsiders.

This type of material is popularly known as trade secrets and know-how. It is commercially valuable and in practice is safeguarded using confidentiality or non-disclosure agreements.

Trade secrets have been described in a recent court case as being secret formulae for the manufacture of products and also names of customers and the goods they buy.

Know-how, although not a legally defined term, is generally understood to include technical information such as drawings, manuals, specifications and designs, for example, of prototypes. This is *technical know-how*.

Commercial know-how relates to ways in which a business operates, its lists of customers, prices and suppliers. Because of the intangible nature of much of this information, practical control of access to others is difficult. However, a certain measure of control is possible and the effects are recognized in the courts.

In the USA, trade secrets (this term as used here also includes know-how) are protected by state law. Although the precise wording of the law varies from state to state, the main features are consistent throughout and encompass information which is of value to the business, is not generally known and is kept as secret within the business as working requirements permit. Although working conditions frequently require that trade secrets must be disclosed to employees, customers, suppliers and others who need to know, this type of disclosure does not destroy its value provided the owner of the secret (usually the proprietor or board of directors) takes precautions to prevent unauthorized access to the information, for example, by restricted file availability, stamping all proprietary information 'Confidential' and entering into written non-disclosure agreements (of the kind set out in Appendix 5).

One word must be said about the difference between trade secrets and other intellectual property rights. A trade secret, unlike a patent, does not need to be novel. It need not be in written form and it is not limited to a particular subject-matter. Furthermore, a trade secret lasts as long as the material remains secret. In this latter respect, protection as a trade secret could have commercial advantages over patent protection for certain areas of technology. Bear in mind, too, that a patent gives a monopoly for at most 20 years and only in those countries where it has been granted and maintained. Furthermore, there is often no other protection available for such material as non-technical business information, including plans, customer lists and other commercially valuable business information, although the holding of lists on databases is being embraced within certain copyright laws.

Confidential information

As we have seen, one of the important criteria for a trade secret to be upheld by a court is that it is kept secret and that the owner has taken all steps reasonable in the circumstances to ensure that it is kept secret by any authorized recipient.

The most usual and effective way of doing this is using a *confidentiality or non-disclosure agreement* either as a free-standing agreement or used, within a contract, as a confidentiality undertaking. As both forms use the same basic restrictive wording, it will be useful to indicate what must appear in such an agreement. Because of the importance of this type of non-disclosure commitment – made expressly (or impliedly) by contractual obligation – Appendix 5 sets out a specimen confidentiality agreement which you may find useful under conditions where a more complex agreement cannot be prepared: for example, on a trade mission where you do not have your legal adviser with you.

Because the confidentiality agreement plays such an important part during the early stages of disclosure and negotiation, it is useful to consider the *requirements for a confidentiality agreement*.

- Date of the agreement.
- Name and address and official capacity of each party.
- Definition of the project, or technical area, in broad terms.
- Undertaking by both parties to keep secret and confidential all information disclosed.
- Receiver to use information only in respect of the project.
- Receiver to restrict dissemination to employees on a 'need-to-know' basis, with corresponding confidentiality undertakings.
- Information to be returned if no further working agreement is reached.
- Confidentiality undertaking not to apply to that which was known to the receiver at the time of disclosure; which is in the public domain; or which becomes legally known to the receiver subsequently without a confidentiality undertaking.
- Undertakings to survive after termination of the agreement and until the information legitimately passes into the public domain.
- Law applying (English or perhaps more conveniently the law of the state of the US party).
- Signature of both parties and date.

5   Product Liability

History and overview of strict liability

The current American law of strict liability, or liability without fault, has its origins in the Middle Ages, when authorities in thirteenth-century England published statutes pertaining to food purity. In subsequent centuries, the concept of strict liability extended beyond food to include medicines.

Today, the concept of strict liability in the USA has broadened to include all manner of goods, where a seller must stand behind his goods. To appreciate the significance of the concept of strict liability, it is necessary to consider both the law and the underlying social policy.

US law

The rule is comprehensively stated in section 402A of the Restatement of Torts. This rule states:

402A. SPECIAL LIABILITY OF SELLER OF PRODUCT FOR PHYSICAL
HARM TO USER OR CONSUMER

(1)   One who *sells any product* in a *defective condition unreasonably
dangerous* to the user or consumer or to his property is
subject to liability for physical harm thereby caused to the
ultimate user or consumer or to his property, if
   (A)   the seller is *engaged in the business* of selling such a
product, and
   (B)   it is expected to and does reach the user or consumer
without substantial change in the condition in which it
is sold.

(2)   The rule stated in subsection (1) applies although
   (A)   the *seller has exercised all possible care* in the preparation
and sale of his product, and
   (B)   the user or consumer has not bought the product
from or entered into any contractual relation with the
seller.

There are five aspects to consider in the definitions. The first
phrase of note is *sells any product*. While this phrase means
exactly what it says, it also includes components of a product,
and the store owners and other vendors who *do not* manufacture
products. It is anyone who sells any product.

The second phrase to consider is *unreasonably dangerous*. This
is a relative term, and impossible to confine to any one context.
Essentially, it means any product which is in a defective condition not contemplated by the ordinary consumer – a question
involving society's expectations and common usage. Consider
that many products cannot be made safe in all applications.
Ordinary sugar is poisonous to a diabetic. That does not make
sugar unreasonably dangerous. Glass can break, and when it
does it can cause serious injury. That does not mean that glass
must be excluded from general use. Finally, even life-saving
drugs usually have side effects. That does not make particular
drugs unreasonably dangerous. The burden of proof to show
that a product is unreasonably dangerous falls on the plaintiff.

Again, it is a trade-off, with society's expectations and the social utility of a product balanced against possible unsafe conditions.

Safe conditions go beyond the product itself and include packaging and instructions or warnings. A product that normally is considered safe can become unreasonably dangerous if it has inappropriate instructions or warnings on it. Conversely, a product which many would consider inherently dangerous may be found not to be unreasonably dangerous if it has appropriate warnings and instructions with the packaging.

Unreasonably dangerous also includes the concept of expected use, and this includes foreseeable misuse. If a seller can reasonably foresee misuse of a product, he is obliged either to design around that foreseeable misuse or attach suitable warnings and instructions to discourage it. A classic illustration is the power lawnmover. Incredibly, there are certain people who believe that power lawnmowers are appropriate tools for trimming hedges. We know this. It is a foreseeable misuse of power lawnmowers. There are other people who believe that it is perfectly acceptable to clean the lawn mower chute while the engine is running – another foreseeable misuse. As a result, the power lawnmower industry recognized the misuse, and redesigned the lawnmowers to avoid these problems. In the USA they all now have 'deadman' features so that if one lets go of the handle, it automatically turns off. This feature makes it extremely difficult to clean the chute while the engine is running, just as it makes it very difficult to use the mower as a hedge trimmer.

The next phrase to consider is *engaged in the business of selling*. This simply means that one has to be in the business of selling to become strictly liable. If A buys a new car and decides to sell his old car to his next-door neighbour, who takes it out for a drive and the brakes fail and he crashes the car, A is not liable under section 402A of the Restatement of Torts because he is not in the business of selling cars. A may, however, be liable under other theories. Similarly, if a lady bakes a cherry pie to sell at the PTA sale and there is a cherry-stone cooked into the pie and someone who purchases the pie breaks a tooth, that lady is not liable under section 402A because she is not in the business of baking and selling pies.

Another phrase to be considered is *without substantial change in the condition in which it is sold*. This means that if the product is substantially changed after it leaves the seller's hands, and the change results in accident or injury, the seller is not responsible. However, foreseeable misuse is included in the concept of unreasonably dangerous, and if the change in the product which occurs after the sale is foreseeable, the seller may not escape liability. For instance, a manufacturer sells a machine to an employer. The employer puts it on the production line where, under pressure to increase production, he disengages various safety devices on the machine. In addition, the employer may instruct the employees to operate the machine in an unsafe fashion to spur production. Theoretically, these kinds of activities should relieve the seller of liability in the event of an employee injury when using the machine. However, if the misuse by the employer was foreseeable by the seller, he may not escape liability. Packaging, labels and warnings must all be considered. If an employer or employee misuses or causes the misuse of a product and it can be shown to be the result of improper packaging or instructions, the seller will not escape liability.

Finally, there is the phrase *the seller has exercised all possible care in the preparation and sale of his product*. This means that even though the seller has done everything possible to sell a safe product, he can still be held liable because fault or negligence is not an element of strict liability. The seller is responsible if a product is unreasonably dangerous when it leaves his hands and it causes an injury.

Contributory negligence on the part of the consumer is not a defence. Assumption of risk, that is, the voluntary and unreasonable encountering of a known danger, can be a defence but is a difficult one to prove.

Typically, when a person is injured, he will sue his immediate vendor. That vendor then has a cause of action against his vendor and so on up through the chain of distribution to the manufacturer, assuming that it is a manufacturing or design defect.

In recent years, product liability law has gone to the extreme in most of the USA, but the pendulum is beginning to swing in the other direction. Many state legislatures as well as the Federal

Congress are acting to put some limits on product liability or strict liability concepts. For instance, in Illinois, plaintiffs can no longer plead punitive damages as a matter of course. They must be able to demonstrate *a reasonable likelihood of showing facts* to support wilful and wanton conduct that would justify punitive damages. Plaintiffs may not so plead if they are more than 50 per cent responsible.

Other states have enacted statutes of repose which bar actions against a product a certain number of years after the product was produced or sold. At least 45 states have passed or introduced bills putting caps on pain and suffering and other non-economic loss damages. In addition, joint and several liability among defendents is undergoing scrutiny.

The comparative position in the UK

Having considered the law in the USA it may be useful to look briefly at the present position in the UK to appreciate the significance of the differences.

There are three areas of law in the UK under which manufacturers and suppliers of goods may have liabilities in respect of defective products. These are the law of contract, the law of tort and, under statute, the Consumer Protection Act 1987 and, before that, various statutes including the Sale of Goods Acts 1893 and 1979. This body of law relating to the rights and defences open to both manufacturers and consumers/purchasers of defective products is one of the most complex in the world.

Under the law of contract there must be a direct link between the contractual obligation, the defect and the damage. Under the law of tort, negligence features prominently if a breach of an established duty of care resulting in damage can be proved. In respect of product liability brought about by breach of statutory regulations, the liability of manufacturers and suppliers under the Consumer Protection Act 1987 is in addition to their responsibilities under the laws of contract and tort and other existing statutory regulations. Under the 1987 Act, a person who is injured or whose personal property is damaged by a product will be able to claim against the manufacturer and/or the supplier of the product if it can be shown that the product was defective. There are, however, various defences to a claim of product liability under the Act, and these defences result in a liability which is significantly less than in the USA which, as we have seen, includes strict liability – that is, liability without fault.

Preventative management

In the ordinary course of events, manufacturers and sellers cannot escape the application of strict liability, but manufacturers in particular can establish certain safeguards to reduce their exposure. The following are certain 'preventative management' ideas:

Anticipate product misuse or abuse

This is a design phase consideration, with classic examples in various industries. Paraffin heaters is an example. When oil prices skyrocketed, the use of paraffin space heaters rose dramatically in the USA. At the same time, the incidence of fires and other injuries due to the improper use of paraffin heaters also rose dramatically. Since then, paraffin heaters have been largely redesigned to anticipate and discourage known abuse of the product, and as a result injuries and fires have been reduced.

At the other end of the scale are all-terrain vehicles. There have been over 275,000 serious injuries and almost 700 deaths resulting from the use of these three-wheeled all-terrain vehicles. At least half of these deaths have been children under 16 years of age. Such deaths and injuries are well documented yet, until recently, the manufacturers insisted that they had produced a safe product and that they were not going to change it. While there are some indications that these manufacturers are softening their position, it is also evident that it is poor economics to wait for regulation and lawsuits to force a redesign of products. The manufacturer is wiser to anticipate potential misuse or problems, recognize them when they are in the market-place and then take steps to redesign the product.

Document each stage of product development
There are two schools of thought on document retention in the manufacturing sector, and a decision on this issue will depend on the specific industry, product and market. One view is that it is important and useful to thoroughly document the product, its development, its design and its production, and then maintain those documents. Another view is that it is better to implement very short document retention policies, thereby minimizing the number of files that are maintained by the company and which would be open to discovery by a plaintiff's lawyer in the event of litigation. Discovery of documents is a procedure of the court whereby each party is obliged to reveal all documentation in its possession regarding the matter under investigation.

As a general rule, it is probably better to document and maintain files on the design and production of the product. For example, one case involved a blowtorch manufacturer who was experiencing problems in the field. The blowtorches were 'blowing off' when in use by the welders. Inspection indicated that the valve cores used in the manufacture of the blowtorches were inadequate and it was the valve core which was failing, causing the blowout and the unregulated flow of gas to the flame. The manufacturer, alleging serious damage in the market-place, sued the valve core producer. Upon discovery and after receiving appropriate documents, it was clear that the valve core producer did not sell the faulty valve cores to the blowtorch manufacturer. Many years previously, the valve core producer had sent to the manufacturer samples of this particular valve core for testing with specific gases, free of charge. A document was discovered stating, 'here are a thousand valve cores free for testing by you in this particular application'. The manufacturer had simply taken the valve cores, put them in the blowtorches, and sold the torches without doing any testing and without indicating that only specific gases should be used. Because of personnel turnover and the fact that the passage of time blurs everyone's memory, it would have been very difficult to prove those facts if the file documents had not been maintained.

Identify critical components
Wherever possible, the file that is maintained on the product should identify the critical components in the product and, in turn, the critical components should be labelled as such when they are part of the final product. In this way, if there is a lawsuit, the lawyer can then establish whether or not it was his client's product that injured the consumer. If one examines the product carefully and knows in advance what the critical components are, it can frequently be established that somebody replaced one of those critical components with a different component which may not have been installed correctly or matched specifications. Any of these items could relieve the manufacturer of liability. Even if the product which injured the person contained all the original components, if a particular component failed, the manufacturer of the product may be able to involve the component manufacturer if that was the actual cause of the injury, and thereby avoid liability.

Design and manufacture in accordance with national and local codes of standards
A foreign manufacturer of products should ensure that its product complies with all state and federal design and manufacturing codes.

Clearly identify rated capacity and foreseeable significant misuse
By clearly identifying rated capacity and appropriate use of the product, a manufacturer can avoid damage to the product as well as personal injury to users of the product. It also greatly aids in the defence of the case if there is an injury. It is important to remember, however, that it does not help to identify rated capacity if your salesmen disregard that information and sell the product for use at a greater capacity.

Adequate instructions and warning
If a product has what could be considered 'inherent' hazards, the manufacturer can attempt to minimize those with instructions and/or warnings. In addition, the products should be sold with safe installation and operating instructions as well as instructions on cleaning, repairs and replacement parts. Warnings are a difficult subject, and obviously depend a great deal on the product and the market-place. However, there are some general rules about warnings:

- they must be designed to catch the user's attention;
- they must be understandable to the ordinary person;
- they must clearly describe the danger;
- they must describe how to avoid it.

Warnings should not try to minimize or obfuscate the danger.

Advertising
Advertising should be reviewed by both those involved technically and legal counsel. In order to avoid any potential allegation that a hazard was misrepresented or concealed in the advertising, all advertisements should be examined for exaggerated claims of performance or inaccuracies regarding safety. Any photographs or illustrations of the product should be current, and they should show the product being used with all safety features in operation. For example, it would be foolish to show a young girl in shorts operating a metal-cutting machine if safe operation requires protective clothing, safety goggles and so on.

Another example is that of a young man who bought a sports car and, unfortunately, chose to drive it at speeds topping 100 miles an hour across the top of a levee. The car became airborne, flipped over several times, and killed the young man. His family sued the car manufacturer, to which the manufacturer countered by stating that the car was not being used properly – who in his right mind would drive a car at speeds in excess of 100 miles an hour on top of an uneven levee? The plaintiff's lawyer had a very simple response: he subpoenaed the car dealership, which had a VCR with a monitor on which they ran a video tape showing this particular sports car in action. On the tape, the car drove along at high speed on curving, bumpy roads, burst over the crests of hills, became airborne, and skidded to a stop. Finally, a beautiful girl sauntered to the car to discuss its merits with the driver. The plaintiff's lawyer argued that the young man, by seeing this advertising, was led to believe that the tape depicted an appropriate use of the car, and he won the case. Advertising can be dangerous.

Dealer and distributor follow-up

Be sure that dealers and distributors are selling the product with manuals and warnings, and are not varying the rated capacity information. Check that they are selling the products properly assembled and ensure that they are discussing the products appropriately. Again, the all-terrain vehicle is a classic example. It is well known that ATVs are especially dangerous with a passenger on the back. Supposedly, dealers and sellers were warned on that point and told that buyers should be apprised of the danger to passengers. A television programme did a story that spotlighted the dangers of ATVs. A hidden camera was installed in a van and the van driven to a dealership, where a man wearing a concealed microphone went in and pretended to be a purchaser. He told the dealer that he wanted to buy ATVs for his two pre-teen children, and he specifically asked whether it would be safe if they took their friends for a ride. The dealer said, 'Yes, no problem.' Obviously, as the programme graphically illustrates, this was asking for trouble. As an additional safeguard, check to make sure that your dealer and distributors have the requisite insurance.

Field service reports

Field service reports can serve a defensive function, and should cite the day, time and nature of work done. Any unsafe or defective conditions or uses should be noted by the field service representative, who should then ask the user to sign the report to show that he has been notified. If a problem occurs later, then the manufacturer can show that they specifically pointed out this misuse of the product which was acknowledged by the user, who then continued at his own risk.

Liaison between departments

Safety, research, engineering, production, legal, sales and insurance are all facets of a plan to maximize preventative management. The exchange of information in the proper implementation of your programme is critical, not just initially, but through any improvements or changes to the product or to its packaging. Any time there is a change to the product, the manufacturer should ensure that the sales materials, packaging and advertising are still accurate and current.

Sales contracts

Manufacturers can attempt to minimize their exposure through their contractual documents. Such measures have little impact with regard to the injured consumer. However, they can serve to limit exposure to others in the chain of distribution. Furthermore, sales organizations should check their contracts to make sure that they are not accepting additional liability and, if they are, should be insured to cover it. The other side of the coin is that liability may be passed on contractually through hold harmless or indemnity clauses.

Disclaimers and warranties

Disclaimers and warranties on invoices and other sales documents are not generally effective regarding injured consumers. However, they can narrow liability to others in the distribution chain, provided employees are clearly instructed to use the forms at all times.

Intracorporate communications concerning products

Product communications fall into four general areas: design; manufacturing; marketing; and claims.

In general, all employees should assume that every document is going to be 'discovered' and used against the employer in litigation, discovery of documents being a procedure of the court whereby each party must reveal all documentation regarding the matter under investigation. Obviously, then, employees should be careful about what they write. For example, an employee's concerns about the safety of a product design should be discussed with a supervisor. If an employee does create a document, the supervisor should respond to it in writing, thus avoiding the discovery of unanswered memos expressing safety concerns.

Once a product is designed, a complete product history file should be established, and kept under the control of one person. Blueprints and specifications should be included along with the other paperwork connected with product development, manufacturing and marketing. If a product is modified, the associated paperwork should be included in the file. In the event of litigation the company's lawyer can easily review the product file and take appropriate action. How long such a product file is maintained will depend on the life of the specific product and its potential hazards. When a product is marketed, warnings on instructions can lead to undue exposure and should be carefully assessed. The company should also make sure that appropriate disclaimers of warranty language are included in bold type as part of the terms of sale forms.

Proper procedures should be implemented to ensure that those forms are used regularly by all divisions, and that they are used in such a way that a court would be likely to uphold the language on the company's forms.

Another area for concern is the 'in-house' memorandum. A manager, salesman or executive sending a letter beyond the company's walls will review it and possibly revise it several times before it is sent. The final draft is carefully considered. In-house or 'to the file' memos are frequently less carefully considered. Internal memos are often penned when there are conflicting opinions within the company as to the best course of action. Subsequently, when company policy has been determined and acted upon, litigation may occur. These memos, if discovered, can be used with devastating effect by plaintiffs to cross-examine the wisdom of the company's decision. Such memos should therefore be discouraged.

When a claim is made or threatened, it should be assessed and a determination made as to whether there is insurance cover or other support (indemnification, contribution). Notification provisions should be followed.

Reports concerning claims should be oral where possible. All employees should keep the preceding suggestions in mind if they are committing anything to paper, and should be cautioned about writing about matters which are pure speculation or rumour without clearly identifying them as such. Similarly, employees should be careful not to report the claimant's story as 'the facts'. Employees should be aware that in these situations the facts may take a long time to uncover.

Insurance against liability claims

Although various measures can be taken to reduce the risk to both manufacturers and suppliers, there is a residual exposure for anyone introducing products into the market-place. The consequences of this exposure can be reduced very considerably by product liability insurance, which plays a key role in risk management strategy in relation to product liability exposure.

If risk management planning is to achieve its goal it is necessary to have a clear understanding of the scope and limitations of product liability insurance. Chapter 6 describes the insurance cover which is available to both manufacturers and suppliers, and looks into the practical aspects of obtaining adequate liability insurance and how a suitable programme can be structured to achieve the desired protection internationally. Such cover is necessary in view of recent decisions in the US courts where juries, unlike the courts of the UK (and Europe), hear civil cases including product liability, and have awarded multi-million-dollar sums against defendant manufacturers of defective products. The availability of product liability insurance and the protective cover it provides is therefore extremely important to both manufacturing and distributing companies, with their inevitable risk and exposure to product liability claims.

The need for manufacturers, distributors, wholesalers and retailers to have adequate insurance cover within the product liability areas of the law can be argued to be greater today than at any time in the history of US product liability law.

Fortunately, industry now enjoys the position in which there is available comprehensive general liability insurance, which specifically includes product liability insurance, and gives protection against claims for bodily injury and property damage instituted against firms in the complex distribution chain from manufacturer to ultimate user.

6 Insurance

The company at risk

Any form of trading puts you as a sole trader or partner of your company at risk. Because the cost of a legal action is high and frequently takes a number of years, the effects on both you and your company have been expressed by many as 'devastating'.

When you trade in the USA the relevance of this statement is even greater. No longer can you avoid the issue by saying, 'it cannot happen to me'. In the USA, as elsewhere, legislation continues to increase and it becomes increasingly likely that one day you or your company will be faced with the debilitating effects of a court case. It may be one which has been brought against you or it may be one which you have to bring against another company to protect your position or to defend your rights.

The effects when this happens can be far reaching and the consequences can prove to be very damaging. In addition to the psychological effect, the time lost and the effort wasted, there are the serious consequences associated with the cost of the litigation process. In the USA these costs can be very high: for example, a patent infringement suit can cost as much as £750,000 to resolve; a product liability suit could be much higher, with the risk of crippling damages in the event of losing the case. (In the USA you are frequently in the hands of a jury which tends to favour the individual who usually appears to have suffered at the hands of the larger company.) Lawsuits of this dimension can adversely affect not only your capacity to trade but also your standing as a trader, and can affect cash flow. Maintenance of liquidity becomes difficult and insolvency suddenly looms on the horizon.

Taking out *commercial insurance* to protect, for example, buildings, staff and goods in transit is normal commercial practice. In the same way, the practice is increasing of having corporate insurance cover for legal expenses in the event of employment disputes, leasing disputes, tax proceedings and also to protect you personally against legal proceedings against you as a director or officer of the company. There are also the insurances concerned with transport and cover for your export credit risks.

Transport insurance – cargo covers your risk when goods are transported to customers in the USA and is one which you will have already encountered trading with other countries. The type of insurance and extent of cover will depend upon the shipping contract and terms of delivery. For an FOB (free on board) contract, you are the owner of the goods until they pass over the side of the ship's rail – you are therefore responsible for loss up to the time goods are loaded but not subsequently. You must ensure that the importer understands this and has adequate insurance. In the case of a CIF (cost, insurance and freight) contract, you as exporter are responsible for the goods during transit and so must have a more extensive insurance cover. Other insurance covers are available, the most expensive being all-risk coverage, but you must seek advice from the freight forwarder or a marine insurance broker. Help with addresses is given in Appendix 9.

Credit insurance ensures that you as an exporter will be paid for your goods. The most effective way to do this is to insure against any loss you may suffer in the event that your customer is unable to pay. This insurance will not be necessary if you can arrange to be paid cash in advance or by a confirmed irrevocable documentary letter of credit. However, if the letter of credit is unconfirmed or payment will be by draft or bill of exchange, or if you deal in an open account, you may find that you do not receive payment for your goods perhaps because the overseas buyer defaults or he becomes insolvent. It is in these circumstances that it would be prudent to insure against non-payment.

You can obtain export credit insurance from a number of places. The official credit insurer in the UK is the Export Credits Guarantee Department (ECGD). This insurance agency is responsible to the Board of Trade and has the full backing of government resources. As well as providing the credit insurance you are seeking, the ECGD provides loan support to banks and project financing for exporters. You can also obtain your export credit insurance from the private sector.

No longer, however, is it impossible to obtain insurance for legal actions that have started. There is now an insurance which is directed to financing and funding continuing actions. This litigation insurance provides insurance cover to meet a litigant's cost in pre-existing and continuing commercial litigation. It can provide security for bank lending or when so required by the court.

The advantages of being able to obtain cover for existing litigation are clear. You have a known finite premium instead of an unquantifiable liability, with financial muscle to see litigation through to its conclusion and the assurance that opponents take your case seriously and will consider early settlement. You are placed in a much stronger bargaining position.

There are other important areas of your business which often go unprotected. One concerns your product and the legal right you have to prevent others from making or selling that product. In other words, you need insurance to help pay the legal costs should you be in a position to defend your *intellectual property rights* – whether in the form of patent, trade mark or copyright – to prevent others from copying or trading in breach of the monopoly right you have.

You may also find that the launch of your product in a new territory is challenged by a third party alleging infringement of their rights.

But you may also experience the problems of injury or bodily harm resulting from the use of your product by your customers. This area of legal liability – *product liability* – is one which is of great importance throughout the world, but particularly in the USA.

Intellectual property rights insurance

'It is probably fair to say that the most significant area of legal practice to have emerged in the last ten to fifteen years has been intellectual property. . . . Indeed, these days it is often the case that the real value of a company will lie in its IP rights, rather than the bricks and mortar of its buildings, or its stock in trade.'

The Legal 500

It is only relatively recently that insurance has become available in the areas of infringement of intellectual property and product liability claim which is within the financial reach of even small to medium-sized companies.

Let us first consider intellectual property rights insurance. There are few businesses that do not use, or make use of, intellectual property. The manufacture or sale of a product, be it for household or industrial use, involves patents, trade marks, design rights or copyright. If you hold any of these rights they give you a commercial advantage which you must be able to defend if someone challenges or infringes your rights. In the USA alone, infringement actions approach 1000 per annum, while in the UK the number is fast approaching 200 per annum. Whether or not you hold any of these rights, the mere manufacture or sale of a product may infringe someone else's rights, with potentially disastrous financial consequences. A challenge that you cannot afford to defend yourself against could affect your profitability or, at worst, close your business down.

If the business has activities in design, publishing or information technology involving videos, computer software or recording material, copyright infringement is a real possibility as this area of intellectual property is nebulous, often difficult to identify and therefore a more difficult one in which to protect your rights. Additionally, activities on e-mail and the Internet make a business particularly vulnerable.

Prudent worldwide searches for other party's intellectual property rights cannot ensure that you will not infringe, while careful protection of your ideas through registration of patents, trade marks or designs will not prevent infringement if there is a determination to infringe.

The cost of pursuing infringers is high: in the USA the cost of a full infringement action can be as much as $1 million (though the cost of defending yourself against alleged infringements with the possibility of damages being awarded against you can, in total, be considerably higher). Unless you have funds available to finance litigation you may have no alternative but to curtail your manufacture or sales programme.

Historically, insurance has only been available to cover legal costs and expenses and was only available to owners of intellectual property rights wanting the ability to enforce them. Insurance available from the UK frequently excluded infringements occurring in the USA, and, if not a total exclusion, restricted the limits of indemnity and usually included a high excess or co-insurance payable by the insured. Those available from the USA, such as the cover offered by Homestead through Intellectual Property Insurance Services Corporation, were restricted to the pursuit of infringers of your own intellectual property rights and carried a 25 per cent co-insurance with an indemnity limit of $500,000, but IPIS Corporation also now offer other policies, including protection against your alleged infringement of other parties' intellectual property rights.

If you are active in the USA and have a base there, the advantages of having a policy with a US carrier (underwriter) with experience of intellectual property litigation are obvious. Equally obvious, however, are the disadvantages of such a

US-based policy if the indemnity levels are low and if you are a UK-based company.

The solution to this problem has been found by a leading UK insurance broker which has facilities to offer a US intellectual property insurance policy as part of the revolutionary policy it has developed with Lloyd's as underwriters. This policy offers the possibility of worldwide cover for UK-based and US-based business, a high level of indemnity and the possibility of a very low excess.

This new facility, offered by FirstCity Insurance Brokers Limited, a Lloyd's broker, reimburses your agreed legal costs should you need to challenge an infringer or should you need to defend yourself against allegations of infringement of the intellectual property rights of others, with the option of an extension to include damages awarded against you. You can also protect yourself against the legal costs of acting against a licensee if the terms of the licence agreement are breached; this extension of the policy also covers breach of terms of a confidentiality or non-disclosure agreement. When your operations extend beyond the UK into mainland Europe, into the USA and Canada or even worldwide, all aspects of the insurance cover are available.

The FirstCity innovative approach is based on a 'module' principle which is designed to meet the needs of businesses for the future:

MODULES

Section A   Provides insurance for agreed legal expenses for pursuing infringers of your intellectual property rights (copyright, because of its increasing importance commercially and the problems associated with defining portfolios, has a module of its own), as well as defending any counterclaim.

This is important for protecting the value of your intellectual property rights.

Section B Provides insurance for agreed legal expenses for defending yourself against allegations of infringement of the intellectual properly rights of others when you manufacture or sell your products (including copyright).

This is very important, as even the best searches in the world will not guarantee that no prior right exists.

Section C Provides insurance for agreed legal expenses for pursuing infringers of your declared copyright.

Vital for those working in the publishing/media industries.

Section D Provides insurance for agreed legal expenses for pursuing a breach of terms of an agreement where your technology is licensed to others or is disclosed under written confidentiality agreements

Important to you whatever your industry, especially if your licensee is on another continent.

Section E Provides insurance for damages awarded against you following an inadvertent breach of intellectual property rights belonging to others.

While legal costs can be staggering, the damages can be devastating. Many large organizations have paid phenomenal damages: for example, the millions of dollars paid in the Kodak–Polaroid case.

Cover is available for any combination of the above modules. The policy, together with the proposal form, is the basis of the contract with the underwriter. It is most important that the insurance contract does what you want it to do, and the proposal form is in a format which enables you to set out clearly what you want and do not want covered – for example, there could be a single patent or an entire intellectual property portfolio. What you require to be covered is set out in detail in the proposal form, and what the underwriter agrees to cover is set out in the schedule to the policy; 'grey areas' of definition are avoided, giving you confidence to operate in the international market-place. You also have the opportunity to select the amount you are prepared to contribute in the event of a claim. Obviously, the higher the amount of self-insurance (excess), the lower the premium will be. Limits of cover from £100,000 to £20,000,000 can be provided.

Furthermore, because of the involvement of an in-house lawyer/technologist, the brokers are able to discuss and advise on your needs prior to considering an insurance solution. The flexibility of this approach ensures that your interests are best served. The broker can also arrange for an independent team of legal and technical experts to carry out a detailed evaluation of your intellectual property and products. This enables both the company and the potential insurance underwriters to understand fully the exposures that are involved in the insurance cover and requirements.

One further point worthy of special note is the risk you take when you import and sell your product in the USA. Not only ought you to check that you do not infringe a third-party right to avoid the financial and other consequences if you are forced to stop selling, it is also important to follow the directions of article 2 of the US Uniform Commercial Code which states: 'unless otherwise agreed, a seller who is a merchant regularly dealing in goods of the kind warrants that the goods shall be delivered free of the rightful claim of a third person by way of infringement or the like.' Searches of the patent literature can be carried out by skilled patent lawyers (called a patent infringement search), but in the USA in particular this can leave material uncovered. The risk of infringement is consequently higher in the USA than elsewhere and warrants insurance protection.

Product liability insurance

We have already considered in Chapter 5 the consequences of introducing a new product to the market-place and how the

effect of harm caused by the use of the product can be minimized.

No matter what steps you have taken to ensure that the
product is safe to use, someone could allege harm and commence an action against you for damages. Fortunately, you are
able to protect yourself against these risks by taking out product
liability insurance. Although such an insurance must be paid
for, the cost is only one of many factors to be taken into account
when setting the price of the goods. No trader, whether manufacturer or retailer, should be without product liability insurance
– this applies particularly in the USA, where we have seen that
the level of damages awarded can be cripplingly high.

A product liability insurance contract is a promise made by
the insurer to make good certain defined losses suffered by the
insured following the use (or misuse) of his product, in return
for a premium paid by the insured. This insurance forms part
of the risk management planning *prior to* the introduction of the
product into the market place.

In the USA the responsibility of the manufacturer along the
entire distribution chain to the retailer is viewed very seriously,
and in consequence with the principle of strict liability, the
level of indemnity must be correspondingly high. There may
therefore be certain advantages in using US underwriters if your
product (or your component in a product) is to be used there,
but there is now a trend for UK underwriters to provide the
necessary high levels of indemnity.

One thing, however, must be emphasized – there is no legal
requirement for a manufacturer to insure in respect of product
liability risks. There are good arguments for making this type
of insurance compulsory – just as insurance is compulsory for
using a motor vehicle on the road and, in most cases, for
employers.

Numerous policies are available in the UK for product liability insurance: for example, from AIG and Chubb. There are
problems associated with underwriting the risk for product
liability, largely because two factors play an important part:
first, the technical assessment and evaluation of the product, its
manufacture and its intended uses, and second, a study of any

preventative management carried out by the company and the care taken with intracorporate communications concerning products. Such assessments and evaluations for product liability as well as for intellectual property insurance are carried out by a few specialist firms, one of which is LBT Services, Poole, Dorset, England.

Some European underwriters provide product liability insurance as part of a package embracing employers' liability insurance and public liability insurance. The employers' liability insurance protects you, the employer, against your liability to compensate an employee who is killed, injured or contracts a disease while working for you, while public liability insurance protects you against your liability to pay damages to anyone, other than employees, accidentally killed or injured while on your premises. Product liability insurance, however, protects you against accidental damage to persons or property arising from a defective product you manufacture or supply.

Although product liability insurance can be obtained as worldwide cover, certain territories, usually the USA and Canada, are frequently excluded or, if not excluded, result in a disproportionately high premium being charged. Any territorial limitation of product liability must be regarded with extreme caution, because it is by no means unknown for a company to be involved in an action under product liability in the USA without any knowledge of having exported there. As an illustration of this principle, if a manufacturer makes a product which can be incorporated in a larger article, for example, a switch in drilling equipment, he will be at risk under product liability law if the drilling equipment is sold in the UK and taken to the USA or merely sold in the UK and then taken for demonstration purposes to the USA; where bodily injury arises as the result of a defect, an action could arise in the USA.

A number of factors are important concerning the contractual limitations in product liability insurance. Some of the more significant clauses in a typical policy are given below:

1   The insurance applies to 'bodily injury' and 'property

damage' only which is caused by an 'occurrence' that takes place in the territory covered.

2 The bodily injury or property damage must occur during the policy period.

3 There are numerous exclusions, falling into categories of risk which are not insurable. These include deliberate acts on the part of the insured; those risks insured under other policies, such as injury to an employee in the course of employment; those risks viewed as particularly hazardous, such as arising out of inhalation or body absorption; those risks connected with asbestos; injury or damage relating to the discharge, dispersal, release or escape of pollutants, including waste material.

4 The Limits of Insurance are shown in the Declaration at the end of the policy as signed and accepted by you, the insured, and these limits fix the maximum amount the underwriters will pay irrespective of the claims made under a typical product liability insurance policy in the USA.

5 Territory for a typical product liability insurance in the USA means the USA, Puerto Rico and Canada. Under certain circumstances, if the injury or damage arises out of goods or products made or sold by you in the USA, Puerto Rico or Canada, the territory is extended to include all parts of the world.

The territorial limits imposed by many underwriters in Europe frequently exclude the USA and Canada or limit the liability in these territories. This restriction must be viewed very critically because, as we have already seen, you frequently have no control over the final destination of your product.

6 Punitive damages are usually excluded. Typical wording is: 'It is hereby understood and agreed that the underwriter's obligation does not apply to fines, penalties, punitive or exemplary damages, in whatsoever form assessed.'

7 Claims occurring, claims made. Most contracts for product liability insurance are on a 'claims made' basis, that is, the policy provides indemnity in respect of injury or damage for claims made by third parties during the period of the

policy. In this way the underwriters are able to control their exposure to claims which could arise in the future, even after termination of the policy.

Under the 'claims occurring' policy, those products which cause undetected injury or damage under a policy can be the subject of an insurance claim at a later date even though the policy was terminated years previously.

It is, however, possible with certain 'claims made' policies to negotiate a retroactive date for the policy.

Layering

One final point of some importance with product liability insurance is the facility for layering. For many risks, the level of indemnity provided by one insurer may not be sufficient. A higher level of indemnity may be obtained by arranging for a number of insurers to each accept a certain level of risk. This is usually arranged by excess layering, such as a primary insurer accepting, for example, $5 million liability while a second insurer will accept a further $5 million liability. In this way high levels of indemnity can be achieved.

7 Trading Arrangements

Before you commence trading with the USA there are two basic decisions you must make.

The first is whether you will operate from your base in the UK and have no formal presence in the USA, or whether you will set up an official trading presence in the USA, controlled by your UK organization.

The second is the legal structure you will trade under. As in the UK there are a number of legal entities open to you, each having specific identifiable advantages and disadvantages.

When you are in the process of making these decisions, it is important to bear in mind that you can export to the USA without establishing an office there, under the legal structure of a sole trader, as a partnership or through your UK company with limited liability. There are advantages and disadvantages to all these entities as we shall see. However, if you do decide to establish a US office, then the question of which legal entity you adopt is a more important one. In the USA there are four basic forms of business structure.

Sole proprietorship

This is an informal structure and the same considerations apply as to a UK sole proprietorship.

The advantages of such an operation are that the business is owned and run by one person. It is less expensive to set up and operate than a partnership, a corporation or a limited liability company. All tax responsibility is with the owner – profits and losses are reported on personal tax returns.

The disadvantages are that the owner has unlimited liability for his business debts, and his personal assets are exposed and put at risk. It is frequently more difficult to obtain finance from the more usual sources such as banks than for the more formal business entities. If you are operating as a sole trader in the UK, you should reassess your position now that you are going to trade in the USA, and should seek legal advice concerning the advantages and disadvantages of changing to company or corporate status.

Partnership

This is an arrangement between two or more parties to work together as co-owners. The arrangement is usually governed by a formal written partnership agreement drawn up between the parties.

In the USA, the legal operation of a partnership is governed by the terms and conditions of the partnership agreement, including financial arrangements and means of dissolution. In circumstances where the wording of the agreement is obscure or the handling of matters under dispute are not included in the partnership agreement, the US Uniform Partnership Act will govern.

The operation of a business as a partnership has certain advantages, including flexibility of operation and low-cost formation and maintenance, but many believe that such advantages are far outweighed by the disadvantage of unlimited liability. In the usual general partnership all partners play an active role and each can bind the partnership by their decisions. The partners carry personal liability for the debts of the partnership which is joint and several, that is, if one partner cannot pay his share of the debt the other partner or partners must pay all the debt.

Corporation

A corporation is a separate legal entity with clearly defined rights and obligations, and it continues irrespective of the presence of individual members. The corporation has its own stockholders (shareholders) and a board of directors, as with a UK company. The officers of the company – president, vice-president, secretary and treasurer – are responsible for the management of the corporation.

The advantages of operating as a corporation over a sole proprietorship or partnership include limited liability of the stockholders and the increased ability to raise finance.

The actual formation of a corporation is governed by the laws of the state in which the corporation is established, preferably in the state in which it is intended to do business or where the headquarters are to be located. A standard incorporation document is filed, following which a certificate of incorporation is issued by the Secretary of State for the state of incorporation.

More detailed information concerning US corporation law is provided in Chapter 12 for those seeking to operate in this way.

Limited liability company

This is a relatively recent extension of corporate structure and is useful as a trading entity for smaller joint ventures and family partnerships. It is not to be confused with a UK company having limited liability. Although the company provides limited liability protection to its members (so-called equity participants) the 'stockholders' are taxed as partners. This avoids the double taxation effect of a corporation.

It is worth noting that a limited liability company can have corporations and partnerships as members and that non-US residents can also be members.

Having decided whether or not to trade with a US presence and established the legal entity for trading, the next consideration is to select the business route which is most acceptable to you, most appropriate to your product and which will achieve your longer-term goal.

There are various alternatives open to you:

- Direct selling
- Agent (manufacturer's representative) or distributor
- Licence arrangement
- Joint venture arrangement
- Franchise

Before looking at each of these alternatives it may be useful to say a few general words on the need for professional advice and guidance, both in the early stages of negotiation and, in the later stages of finalization, where the legal agreement you put in place will have a profound bearing on your operation well into the future.

It is in respect of this area of exploitation that you must have contracts or agreements in place to define the rights and responsibilities of both parties. Because the drafting of these agreements is so critical it is most important that you have professional legal advice from someone skilled and experienced in the commercial legal field (particularly the USA and the UK), someone who can advise you during initial negotiations, draw up the appropriate agreements, and advise you during final negotiations when there may be pressures, either time or finan-cial, to reach an agreed settlement of terms. Skilled negotiations by the other party in the final stages can effectively and unwit-tingly reduce the control you have and can cause you to lose valuable long-term rights for a short-term solution to your problems, such as an immediate cash payment with low subsequent royalties, the payment of which may be vaguely defined.

Because of the importance of these agreements and the need for you to know in advance the areas, both technical and commercial, that you must identify and clearly define during the negotiation of an agreement, a typical distribution and licensing agreement with corresponding checklists are set out in Appendices 1–4. These are examples only – not precedents – and will need professional modification and amendment before they can be tailored to your particular situation. Used in the way they are intended, you will find that you go to the negotiating table much better prepared to make a positive contribution and work as a team with your legal adviser.

Many firms which have successfully traded in the UK, and have then successfully exported into Europe, adopt the method of *direct selling* to US retailers. It is possible to sell directly to customers in the USA without using an intermediary such as an agent, but this route can be difficult to establish. It could be successful for certain industrial goods, however, where you are selling directly to the user, and it could also be successful in certain areas of consumer goods to be sold in department stores and supermarkets.

But the venture will usually achieve more rapid success if you use the services of one of the many representatives established for this purpose and experienced in their field of activity. Such a representative or manufacturer's representative, as is so often used in the USA, may be either an agent or a distributor. Although frequently both terms are used synonymously, particularly in the UK, there are fundamental commercial and legal differences, however, between an agent and a distributor, and it is necessary that these differences are understood.

In establishing the trading alliance with someone in the USA, many firms consider the position they are familiar with in Europe where *distribution* means the appointment of a third party to distribute your product in a defined territory on a buy/sell arrangement and *agency* means the appointment of a third party (agent) to sell your product on your behalf, usually on a commission basis. The same legal difference exists in the USA.

Before deciding whether to proceed with an agency or distribution arrangement it is wise to consider your long-term objectives, how you see your role in handling economic risk during the process, and the involvement and control you wish to have during the trading process. In a distribution arrangement the distributor takes the economic risk, but in an agency arrangement the economic risk remains with you. The distributor buys your product for resale, whereas an agent merely handles it and generally takes a commission on the sale. The agent has virtually no risk if the products cannot be sold. It is important to understand that an agent may play a relatively minor role in the exploitation of a product or service with minimal financial commitment by him, while a distributor frequently has substantial financial investment paying for the initial and subsequent purchases, promotional, marketing and distribution costs, and thus plays a major part in the exploitation.

If you have decided to opt for an agency-type arrangement you will see that there are six basic considerations.

Terms of the relationship

This includes the appointment of an agent on an exclusive or non-exclusive basis in a defined territory for a specified time to carry out defined duties in respect of defined products. Many agents will only enter into exclusive arrangements, but some accept non-exclusive arrangements which become exclusive after satisfactory operation over, say, two years. A good initial time for the agreement is four years, extendible or determinable at notice.

Duties and responsibilities

The responsibilities of both the principal and the agent must be clearly defined to avoid misunderstanding, as this can so often lead to dissatisfaction and breakdown of the working relationship.

Products

Those goods with which the agent is authorized to trade must be defined.

Territory

This must be set out clearly and unambiguously, bearing in mind the complex state structure in the USA.

Fee/commission for agent

Usually straightforward to set on a percentage basis. The issue of reimbursement of expenses may not be so straightforward but must be agreed.

Termination

The agreement should specify those events upon which termination can be effected (for example breach of the agreement, insolvency or liquidation of a party). There should also be an escape clause for both parties operable for a short initial period, say up to six months during which either party may terminate the agreement.

Passing now to those terms and conditions in a distributorship arrangement, somewhat different conditions must be specified in certain areas of the agreement because of the basic difference between your dealings with an agent and with a distributor.

The distributor purchases your products and takes title to them, and sells them to customers in the territory you have allotted to him. The distributor takes much more risk than an agent, and in many circumstances cannot look to you as a principal for indemnification. In particular, he assumes responsibility for bad debts on the sales he makes, and often assumes obligations in respect of warranties, advertising and sales promotion. In return, the distributor has more freedom than an agent and also has a higher rate of remuneration.

There are some important aspects of a distributorship relationship that must be reflected in the Agreement. These include:

1   Exclusive or non-exclusive arrangement. You may have more success more quickly with the grant of exclusive rights.

2   The territory in which the distributor can sell must be clearly defined.

3   Handling and storage of the products. Proper storage of the goods is vital, particularly in areas where there could be extremes of temperature and humidity. You must have a right to inspect the goods at intervals.

4   Sales targets must be set and achieved, particularly if the agreement is an exclusive one. Pricing policies must be agreed. (Also applicable to an agency relationship.)

5   The distributor must be prevented from copying or from modifying the products. (Also applicable to an agency relationship.)

6   Any notices on goods or packaging concerning your patent, copyright or trade mark rights must be left in place.

7   All products must be purchased from you.

8   There must be frequent interchange of views on sales, marketing policies and advertising material. (Also applicable to an agency relationship.)

9   The level of stock held by the distributor must be stated (usually in months' supply).

10   The distributor acquires no right to any of your intellectual property.

11   Clear statements concerning termination of the agreement and those occurrences and events which justify termination of the agreement. Note that each state has its own distributor termination laws, some of which are more onerous than others.

12   The effect of termination and handling of stock held by the distributor.

13   Confidentiality undertakings are important – this would protect the disclosures you make to alert the distributor to any forthcoming modifications or improvements.

14   There must be a schedule of purchase targets to be achieved over defined future periods, with set minimum quantities.

15   The distributor must not manufacture or sell goods which would compete with yours.
16   The terms and supply of your products to the distributor should also be set out, such as delivery, price and payment, fitness of goods, non-liability for delay in delivery.

A checklist useful for negotiations in respect of a distribution agreement is set out in Appendix 1 and a typical distribution agreement, to be used for guidance purposes only, is set out in Appendix 3.

Industrial licensing

Agency and distributorship relationships are primarily concerned with selling a product.

Licensing is primarily concerned with granting rights in respect of technology to be used in manufacture, further research and development, modification, use and assembly. A manufacturer's agent may be useful to help you find someone who would benefit from the grant of a licence.

Parting with technical information can be either by sale or by licence. If sold, for example by assigning your patent or trade mark, you give up all rights in return for a payment. If licensed, you do not give up all your rights to the technology. You may retain the right to use them yourself or license them to others. It is important to specify what rights you are handing over and what rights you are keeping. The licence agreement has as its purpose the setting out in legal terms of those rights that have been granted to the licensee (with any conditions) and those rights that have been retained by you, the licensor.

A checklist for a typical licence agreement involving patents, trade marks, copyright and know-how is set out in Appendix 2, but there are two points which should be highlighted. Because of the technical and legal complexities of a licensing arrangement, a lawyer must be used to prepare any documents which set out the agreement between the parties. The precedent for a general licence agreement is set out in Appendix 4 and is given for general guidance only.

1 There are both advantages and disadvantages to licensing. You have no problems with importation, no transport costs, no adaptation of your domestic product, and minimal commitment of your staff and finances. However, you lose much of your control over marketing and selling policies; your profits are much lower than they would be if you exported your product; your right to sell into the licensee's markets is lost and you run a risk of the licensee later becoming a competitor in other areas of the world – non-competing clauses could be unacceptable in the USA under anti-trust laws.

2 If the agreement is to exclude yourself and others from manufacturing and selling in the licensed territory, it is called an *exclusive* licence. Commercial realities will determine whether or not your grant will be exclusive or non-exclusive. The prospective licensee will frequently insist on exclusivity in order to ensure sufficient market availability to make the start-up manufacturing and market promotional costs of the licensee worth while.

Other considerations of territory, payment (cash only, cash plus annual royalty or royalty only), technology exchange between licensor and licensee, confidentiality undertaking by both parties, safeguarding of patents, trade marks and copyright, termination and handing back information, are all important. In respect of US operations in particular, you, as licensor, must be very wary of what warranties and guarantees you give. A compromise must be arrived at, and this is a critically important area of negotiation.

The two remaining types of association to consider are joint venture and franchise. Because it is regarded by some as a form of licence agreement, it is convenient to review what is understood by the term joint venture.

Joint venture
This is an association between two or more parties (individuals, partnerships or corporations) and is controlled by a contractual agreement setting out the respective contribution by the parties

of skills, knowledge, time, money and resources, and sets out the way in which management and expected profits are to be shared.

A popular type of joint venture is between a manufacturer/exporter in the UK and distributor/importer in the USA. There is usually a sharing of technological information (frequently an intent for the US distributor/importer to manufacture at some time in the future), a sharing of the costs of distribution and marketing, and a subsequent sharing of profits.

Such a joint venture association is frequently established for a longer time than that of a licence agreement. It is frequently set up between parties who have already worked together and often involves larger corporations.

Franchising

Finally, the method of exploitation by franchising must be considered. This has been in operation for more than 20 years in the USA and accounts for more than one-third of all US retail spending.

Franchising is a contractual arrangement between two parties, the franchisor and the franchisee, in which the franchisor gives to the franchisee a right to market and sell specified services or products in a defined territory using the trade mark and know-how of the franchisor and under strict operating standards and procedures. In return, the franchisee will pay a fee to the franchisor, will set up the entire operation as laid down by the franchisor, and will pay the franchisor, on a continuing basis, a percentage of the income. The franchisee normally carries all the liabilities of the business operation.

There are two ways in which you can use franchising to take your ideas into the USA. The first is *direct franchising*, that is, directly selling individual operating units to franchisees. This is only effective if you have already had experience as a franchisor, and have some knowledge of the requirements of such operations in the USA in respect of staffing, day-to-day performance and knowledge of US markets.

The second is *master franchising*, in which you give rights to a US business to operate the franchising for you in the USA. Again, previous experience in the franchising field is essential.

To summarize this mode of exploitation – the risks are lower than the joint venture route; it applies to services and certain products only; it should only be seriously considered by those with previous experience of franchising operations.

8 Entering the US Market

A word of warning on launching a new product into the USA – the American consumer is extremely demanding, and new manufacturers are not given a second chance if their first product fails. Do not use the USA as a test market.

One other warning note concerns the responsibility you have to ensure that your goods are delivered without infringing the rightful claim of any third party. Anyone selling must be aware of his responsibilities and take the necessary action, whether by agreement, searches or otherwise, to ensure that the rightful claim of any third party is not infringed. We have already dealt with intellectual property defence insurance in respect of infringement in the USA in Chapter 6.

Before you can start selling your product in the USA you must set the right price level and you must alert your customers to the availability of the goods and the advantages they have over similar competitive products that are available. You must also bear in mind that if your goods have consumer appeal and sell well, competitive products will appear.

Having set the correct price, how do you make the necessary contacts to disseminate information about your product? There are many routes and a summary of these may give you a guide as to which would be most appropriate. You will need a co-ordinated marketing approach which will inform the public not only of the availability of your product (or service) but price, competitive advantages and, in certain types of goods, repair and maintenance arrangements.

Marketing avenues available to you when trading out of the UK are:

Trade journals
Scientific journals
General technical publications
Federal and state daily and weekly newspapers
Popular periodicals and consumer magazines
Television
Radio
Promotional/trade literature
Direct mailing to targeted areas
Mail order or catalogue
Trade fairs and exhibitions
Telemarketing
Electronic trading
Outdoor posters
Advertising agencies
DTI publications
Yellow Pages directories
Follow-up procedures
DTI and foreign and commercial offices
   Business Link
   Enterprise Initiative
   Export development advisers
   Export promoters
   Market Information Enquiry Service (MIES)
   Export Marketing Research Scheme (EMRS)
   New Products from Britain Service (NPFBS)
   Overseas contacts lists
   North America Outward Mission Scheme
   Trade Fairs Pamphlet Scheme (TFPS)

Seminar organization
Programme-arranging service

Before considering these avenues in detail, a word should be said about the way in which Americans view the concept of advertising. A statistic which is worth mentioning is that the USA spends on advertising almost twice the combined advertising outlay of the major industrial European countries Germany, the UK, France, Spain and Italy – in the region of $10,000 million annually.

One point of note at this stage is the value of establishing trade with Canada as a springboard to entering the USA. Many areas of Canada are very receptive to UK trade and this, combined with the common border between Canada and the USA and their easy trading relationships, offers a wonderful opportunity for phased entry into the USA. With this in mind, your marketing and advertising thrust could perhaps be directed initially to Canada. Trading with a Canadian partner can prove to be a less harrowing way of embarking on trading with the USA. Many Canadian companies and agents/distributors already have trading arrangements in place in the USA and, provided your product fits into their range, will offer your products along with their existing range to their US customers. It is understood that the Canadian Government is providing specific help for this type of springboard operation in at least nine high-tech sectors of industry: advanced software, biotechnology, electronics, geometrics, industrial waste water technology, laser and opto-electronics medical devices, ocean technologies and telecommunication equipment.

We have previously listed the more frequently used channels of product promotion, but these must now be considered individually and their relevance to your category of product highlighted.

Trade journals and general technical publications
These are very good if your products are used in the manufacturing and industrial areas – for example, engine components.
Of equal importance is a press release in such journals or a

short article about the industry and your product's applications. The DTI, through their many press officers and via offices in the USA and embassy and consulates, can frequently help with the initial contacts needed to get an insertion.

Scientific journals

Specialist journals, for example in the field of dentistry, can be used for both advertising material and information/user awareness purposes for a new dental product. There is clearly little point in advertising a dental wax cutting tool in the general press, but an advert (or preferably series of advertisements) in the specialist dental journals can have far-reaching effects. If supported by leading authorities, who use the product success-fully, a technical article on the product can be an invaluable marketing tool.

Newspapers and popular periodicals

Advertisements in the national or in the regional daily or weekly newspapers can be productive of sales if correctly targeted. The *New York Times*, the *Wall Street Journal* and *USA Today* are the major nationwide newspapers, but there are, however, more than 1600 local daily newspapers. It is thus important, particu-larly in the general merchandising areas, to select your territories for advertising. Not only must care be exercised with the territory covered, but also with the frequency for, although relatively inexpensive per shot, if the advertising is to be con-tinued for any length of time the costs can soon become crippling.

The same considerations apply to advertisements placed in popular magazines and periodicals, although here a particular class of consumer can be pinpointed by special interest maga-zines. The circulation and readership of the magazine must be considered – the higher the circulation, the more effective the coverage. Costs can be high, up to $125,000 per colour page for a top, high-readership magazine. For special interest magazines, such as sports and mountain bicycle accessories, the appearance of the advertisement can be timed to coincide with a special event, perhaps an exhibition or trade fair or a sporting championship.

Television

Although there are only a few national TV networks in the USA, there are around 1700 separate TV stations. In order to achieve widespread coverage for consumer products, whether national or regional, broadcast network television is prefered, almost more than 20 million homes being reached by one showing.

For more restricted coverage, one of the 1700 separate TV stations can be used. Audience size is lower than when using broadcast network television, but so are the costs: wide national coverage can cost from $5000 to $500,000 per 30-second commercial, whereas regional cover can be much lower – up to $10,000 per 30-second showing.

Cable network TV is now becoming an important advertising medium and there are more than 30 cable networks running advertising material. Comparative costs are $500 to $10,000.

Radio

The four national radio networks broadcast in such a way that there is both national and regional coverage via syndication to local stations. Local markets are served by spot radio. Costs for a 60-second slot vary considerably – up to $1500 for local spot radio coverage.

Promotional and trade literature/samples

This method of advertising can be very successful if you target your consumers correctly. If it can be linked to a trade fair or exhibition or used as an insert in relevant magazines, much of your potential market can be reached. Trade shows have been shown to be a most useful point of distribution for various forms of advertising material and the demonstration of your product by hand-out samples. The enclosures to letters sent out by trade show organizers can be effectively used to introduce your product on a wide basis.

Direct mail

This can be a most effective means if sufficient time and trouble is taken to target the right consumer. A number of US companies have prepared databases segmenting customers by age, occupation, lifestyle and geographical location. Many mailing lists are available to buy or to rent for virtually any type of customer, and the cost of such lists varies greatly. Some lists can be product related.

You may also wish to market direct to other businesses. Again, such lists are available. A useful source of information on the type and availability of mailing lists is the Direct Marketing Association (DMA) in New York.

Mail order or catalogue

This is a flourishing method of direct marketing, particularly of consumer goods, but it is also becoming increasingly important for industrial goods.

It uses the medium of catalogues, of which there are two types: traffic builders and direct-response books. The former are published in conjunction with retail outlets where the goods are available on display. The latter illustrates goods that are available from warehouses. The Export Market Intelligence Centre Library provides lists of catalogues.

Trade fairs and exhibitions

All important trade organizations in the USA have their own annual trade fair or exhibition. Some have more than one a year, usually located in widely separated areas: for example, one in New York and one in California.

Exhibiting at a suitable, targeted trade fair frequently leads to sales, but initially you may find that the cost of exhibiting is outside your budget. The DTI arranges exhibition stands for members and you may be able to exhibit on one such stand. But if you are unable to exhibit on a stand, much can be gained by merely attending and making contact with others.

Distribution and marketing agents frequently attend trade fairs and exhibitions and the direct contacts you make are often very beneficial. It is important to prepare well in advance –

obtain the show catalogue, select certain companies to meet and mail them in advance if possible. Have your own publicity material available.

Telemarketing
This is an area of marketing which is fast outstripping others, and there are many organizations which use telephone means for promoting products. The only one which is increasing at the same rate is electronic trading. It is most effective when used in conjunction with direct mailing using a toll-free (800) number. All enquiries and order-placing can be handled quickly.

Electronic trading
We are living in an age of information exchange by electronic means, with e-mail and superhighway being words frequently heard. Computers have been designed to accommodate the needs of such an exchange upsurge, and in the area of marketing these new means are being increasingly used.

Marketing and advertising agencies
Many companies selling for the first time into the USA find it useful to seek the advice and help of a marketing expert, from both a public relations point of view and when selecting and placing the advertising and marketing material. There are many such organizations, some of which are located in London. Business Link or your local chamber of commerce will be able to help with names and addresses. One organization in Georgia, USA is Access America Information Services, which provides a great deal of information and data useful for anyone intending to sell into US markets. Their address is PO Drawer R, Acworth, GA 30101, USA (Tel. (1) 404 892 1008; Fax. (1) 404 974 1296).

DTI
The DTI can be of real and valuable assistance, particularly in areas of marketing and product introduction. Persistence and tenacity is needed when dealing with it, especially if you are not sure either what you want from it, or what it can provide, as it is a very large organization and it may take a number

of calls to locate the right person or department holding the information you require. Obtain all their leaflets and publicity material first. Decide upon the particular help needed, both subject-wise and territorially. Then approach the DTI with your specific request; a meeting with the appropriate representative is frequently the preferred way.

Let us look briefly at what is available from the DTI – the head office as set out in Appendix 9 can provide regional addresses in the UK.

The overseas trade services   provided by the DTI and the Commonwealth Office include:

1   *Enterprise Initiative*, which provides consultancy help in marketing, design, manufacturing, quality, business planning, financial and information systems.
2   *Export development advisers* are operated by the Chamber of Commerce in conjunction with the DTI. They provide a wide range of advice on selling to and importing into the USA.
3   *Market Information Enquiry Service* provides fast and cost-effectively most of what you will want to know about selling into the USA. This service is run in conjunction with the diplomatic service post in a particular region of the USA.
4   *Export Marketing Research Scheme*, managed by the Association of British Chambers of Commerce for the DTI. It provides assistance and help in many areas, including overseas sales and promotional and related overseas visits.
5   *New Products from Britain Service* provides editorial material on your product to editors and magazines in selected countries, including the USA. It aims to secure coverage of your product in suitable publications in those countries you have selected. Coverage extends through the national and regional press to trade and consumer magazines. Where necessary, for example, in Mexico, translations will be provided.
6   *North America Outward Missions Scheme*. Financial support is provided by the DTI to those firms selected to go in an

organized group, to attend meetings with potential buyers, customers, and agents in the territory visited. The scheme is administered by the DTI's Exports to North America branch.

9 Export and Import

We saw in Chapter 7 the various means of introducing your product into the USA, by direct selling to retailers, using agents or distributors, by licence, franchise and joint venture.

Adoption of the direct selling route will result in considerable involvement by you as an exporter in the methods of trading such as shipping, importation and warehousing, with attendant factors such as customs and tariffs.

If you want to reduce this involvement you may decide to use the services of an agent; many exporters prefer this to using their own resources to sell directly to retailers (many attempting the direct sell route have found it to be too demanding of time, effort and financial resources), and there are many agents available for this work, in both the UK and the USA. You could find an agent based in the UK who will have all the necessary contacts in the USA. Alternatively, you could appoint an agent who is located in the USA.

Finding a representative or agent is not an easy task, but finding a good one with knowledge and experience of trading with your goods and with contacts in all the necessary outlets is even more difficult. Various organizations assist with agent location and are listed in Appendices 9 and 13. However, there are other ways of getting help with selling.

Freight, warehousing, dispatch and administrative facilities
These facilities are offered by a number of UK firms. One such organization is British Shop UK with a base in the West Midlands and a warehouse and offices in North Carolina.

Freight containers leave the UK on a regular basis and will carry your goods, along with others, to a suitably located warehouse in the USA, e.g. North Carolina. The rates charged usually include customs clearance and documentation, brokerage, wharfage and loading in the UK but do not include duty, insurance and the costs of unloading the container and reloading for onward transportation within the USA. Goods can be stored in the US warehouse, usually free for one month then charged thereafter.

Other office services provided by some of these exporting firms include:

- customer service
- liaising with representatives/agents
- mailing/faxing addresses for orders
- obtaining credit references
- credit control and use of collection agencies.

In addition to the warehouse-type facilities, exporting firms frequently make available other services including:

- distributing goods across the USA by container or air shipment
- storage of goods
- providing a base for returned goods
- providing own phone installation answered in your name.

This service means that, in effect, you establish an office in the USA.

Regular set charges for office services are made – this enables you to budget in advance and adjust the price of your goods accordingly. But it is essential to verify the costs and services offered as changes do occur from time to time. The up-to-date position will be set out in the simple contract you sign with the exporting firm. This usually covers a set period, for example, one year, which is then reviewed before extending into a further period.

Resident agent
This will be either an individual or a firm selling for you on a commission basis. The agent may take care of all import and distribution formalities for you.

Wholesalers
They usually handle a range of goods and import through their own agents or buyers in the UK.

Import commission houses
They usually receive goods from you and sell them on for a commission. They can be regarded in much the same way as agents, and are frequently involved in moving your goods after arranging customs clearance.

Import merchants
They buy the goods from you, stock them, and trade independently of you. Such merchants frequently handle goods in a certain territory or in a certain industrial sector.

There are a number of organizations and documented sources of reference you can make use of when selling directly or indirectly to the USA, and these are given in Appendices 9, 12 and 13.
   The more important documentary sources are:

- *Custom House Guide*
- *International Directory of Importers*
- *Directory of United States Importers*
- *American Association of Exporters and Importers Membership Directory*

- *Importers' Manual USA* Very readable but voluminous manual, packed with useful information. Updated annually. Highly recommended for anyone intending to do business seriously in the USA.

Before you can *import* into the USA, you must *export* from the UK. At each of these stages you will incur costs in terms of time and money, as there is a great deal of documentation to attend to. You must also consider what barriers exist to trade – US customs, tariffs, quotas, exchange controls and import restrictions, to mention only a few.

There are numerous issues to attend to when you export, and most exporters agree that the amount of paperwork required before your goods leave the dockside or airport is a nightmare. Having all the necessary documentation correctly prepared is a crucial step in the overall process of export selling. There are three stages in the preparation of the required documents, and at each stage help will be available from the shipper, agent or freight forwarder. A summary of what is required may be helpful, but do seek guidance from your local or regional chambers of commerce.

Export invoice   This is frequently prepared by your agent and is similar to the form of invoice used for domestic distribution. It shows items including terms of sale, means of transport, shipping date, shipping agent, currency, route to be taken. Between four and nine copies will be needed by the shipping agents. This document is an important one in that it is used by the US customs authorities to determine the value of the goods. It is frequently referred to as a commercial invoice. The guide *Importing into the United States* produced by the Department of the Treasury sets out a list of items which are to be included in the commercial invoice, according to the US Tariff Act 1930.

Export packing note   This can also be prepared by your agent and shows the contents of the shipment, number and type of packages (e.g. cartons), and any numbering used on the cartons. Again, four to nine copies may be required.

Shipping note   This, or an equivalent note used to move goods by air, is the document to move your export goods from your factory or warehouse to the point of holding prior to loading. It is also needed to settle port charges and cargo dues.

Bill of lading   This is a most important transport document. It is the formal receipt by the captain of the vessel for the cargo after it has been loaded on board. Bills of lading are negotiable and will be used by banks for goods being paid through a bank. The bill of lading is prepared by the shipping agent. The information continued in a typical bill is given in Appendix 6.

Airbill   This is the equivalent bill of lading for air cargo and contains much the same information as the bill of lading. One important difference is that the airbill is not a negotiable document.

Export customs entry   This is a statement, usually prepared by the agent, describing the goods for customs purposes, and sets out the customs classifications (or harmonized tariff) code.

Customs export manifest   This is a document used by carriers to declare to customs the cargo that they are carrying.

The next stage in the process of getting your goods to the US market-place is that of *importing* into the USA. When your shipment of goods reaches the USA, entry documents for the goods must be handed to the port of entry authority. The goods are not legally entered into the USA until after shipment has arrived, customs have authorized delivery of the goods and duties have been paid. You as importer are responsible for the examination and release of the goods.

   These responsibilities and duties will be taken by the freight forwarding company if authorized by you, or will be taken by your agent/representative or distributor if you have appointed one. Alternatively, if the goods are being supplied directly to a retailer under FOB terms, such that ownership passed on loading, the retailer (now owner of goods) will arrange importation.

Documents needed for importing

Within five working days of arrival of the goods at the US port of entry certain documents must be produced to the importation authorities. These are:

Entry manifest (Customs Form 7533) or the more usual Application and Special Permit for Immediate Delivery (Customs Form 3461)

These are used to satisfy the first entry requirements. Form 3461 is a simple form and, like all import/export documents, is available from freight forwarders or customs house brokers.

Evidence of rights to make entry

This is provided by producing the bill of lading or airbill.

Commercial invoice (export invoice)

This has already been considered.

Pro forma invoice

If the required commercial invoice is not available, a pro forma invoice must be handed over by the importer at the time of entry of the goods into the USA.

Packing list

This is an important document in respect of customs clearance, and is used to check the contents of the shipment. Numerous details of the shipment must be declared in the packing list, including the dimensions and weight of each package, shipping marks and references of exporter and importer. It is important that the goods are packaged and marked in accordance with US customs law, i.e. every article is to be marked with the English name of the country of origin and must indicate to the purchaser in the USA the country of manufacture or pro-duction.

Trading restrictions

All countries impose some form of control to regulate the exporting and importing of goods, largely for the protection of domestic industry as well as the provisions of revenue and the imposition of foreign exchange control.

Although the UK enjoys a good trading relationship with the USA, there are many US laws which are directed to the control and regulation of trade. Most are aimed at protecting American domestic business from unfair foreign competition, and if you export to the USA you must be aware that a number of trading laws exist that impose duties or even exclude certain classes of goods altogether.

The most frequently encountered trade restrictions are *tariff barriers* imposed and regulated by the Tariff Act 1930. In the USA there are three types of customs duties:

- *'Ad valorem' tariffs*. These are based on the value of the goods, generally determined as CIF.
- *Specific duties*. These are based on the weight or size of the goods.
- *Compound duties*. These combine both *ad valorem* and specific duties.

There is also a *merchandise processing fee* which is imposed as a customs users' fee. There is no value added tax in the USA.

You will be able to obtain further information on the duty levied on your goods from your shipping agent or freight forwarder. The duty will be set according to the US Harmonized Tariff Schedule, available from the US Government Printing Office in Washington.

Non-tariff barriers

Barriers may exist which restrict your trading in certain products. The most commonly encountered non-tariff barrier is the *import quota*, which is a quantity control on certain imported goods for a certain period of time.

US import quotas can be divided into two groups: tariff-rate quotas and absolute quotas.

Tariff-rate quotas   provide for the entry into the USA of a specified quantity of a particular product at a reduced rate of duty for a specific period of time. Quantities imported in excess of the designated quantity are charged at higher rates of duty.

Absolute quotas   concern the quantity of goods imported and not the rate of duty. No more than a specified quantity of the relevant product can be imported during the quota period. Goods brought into the USA in excess of a quota can either be exported or warehoused awaiting the beginning of a new quota period.

Full information concerning which goods are subject to quotas is available from the Quota Branch, US Customs Service, Washington, but it may be useful to know that products subject to tariff-rate quotas include milk and cream in certain forms, tuna fish and certain sugars and syrups. Goods subject to absolute quotas include milk and cream in condensed or evaporated form, some butter substitutes, certain animal feedstuffs, ice cream, peanuts, certain cottons and textiles from particular countries.

Pricing policy
The USA has strict anti-dumping laws to prevent imported goods selling at prices that could injure a US industry. If your goods are held to be selling at prices unjustifiably below your prices on your home market, a duty could be imposed which will be equal to the difference between the home market price and the US price.

Import licence
Certain products require an import licence. It is the responsibility of the importer to ensure that goods are correctly imported under licensing regulations, so some knowledge of the existence of such licences is useful. Information concerning import licences can be obtained from your chamber of commerce or your freight forwarder, but the list of goods includes: alcoholic beverages, animals and animal products, certain drugs, firearms and ammunition, fruit and nuts, meat, milk, dairy products,

petroleum and petroleum products, plant and plant products, poultry and poultry products and vegetables.

International trading agreements

The USA is a party to two important international trading agreements which affect trade from the UK to the USA. These are:

- General Agreement on Tariffs and Trade (Uruguay Round) (GATT, now administered by the World Trade Organization (WTO)).
- North American Free Trade Agreement (NAFTA).

WTO (GATT) provides a framework of rules for the conduct of international trade worldwide. NAFTA creates free trade between the USA, Canada and Mexico. However, the trading commitments of these three states under NAFTA is in addition to the commitments they have under GATT.

Let us now look at these two trading agreements and consider the effect they will have on your trade with the USA.

Generally, it has been estimated that WTO will result in increased trading worldwide to the extent of £270 billion after ten years. Tariffs are to be reduced, and there is an agreement that tariffs on 95 per cent of all goods will not be increased. This will bring trading stability. It is expected that the tariffs on goods traded between the European Union and the USA will on average be halved over the next five years.

In addition to goods, the WTO terms also apply to services. This will be important to those firms providing services to the USA, as all trading partners must be treated in the same way. Any measures regulating trade must be non-discriminatory.

These WTO provisions will provide a more secure basis for trading with the USA and should lead to an increase in trade in all areas, both goods and services. Trading will also be made easier because of a resulting clarification of many of the US trading laws, in particular in respect of anti-dumping, subsidies, volume and sourcing restrictions and in areas of the protection of patents, trade marks and copyright.

NAFTA will have its main impact on the three NAFTA

countries, and is not expected to have much visible impact on many UK companies selling into the USA except in the automobile industry and textiles. However, one important consequence will be felt by those UK companies investing in and setting up manufacturing facilities in the USA – the UK company setting up in the USA will immediately gain the benefits that are enjoyed by other US companies.

10 Financing the Investment, Shipment and Tax Considerations

Irrespective of the means by which sales are made into the USA, whether by direct import, a distribution network, joint venture or through a wholly owned company in the USA, the question of how to finance the investment will arise.

Raising initial capital, at least for financing the formation of a company or setting up a distribution network, is generally not too difficult. For example, as we have seen in other chapters, a company can be formed in the USA for as little as $100 and an issued share capital of $20,000 may be adequate to lease an office and pay the first one or two months' expenses. Similarly, appointing distributors may be even less expensive as most of the cost will involve visits to the USA to view the distributor's operations and negotiate the distribution agreement.

Letter of credit/documentary credit

In any commercial enterprise, a seller of goods wants to sell to a buyer as quickly as possible and be guaranteed that the buyer will pay for the goods. Where the buyer and seller know each other or have a long-standing business relationship, the risk to the seller of not being paid for the goods may be minimal. However, where buyer and seller are unknown to each other or possibly are in different countries, there is potential risk on both sides. The buyer wants to ensure that he will receive the desired quantity of goods ordered of the expected quality, and at the required time and place of delivery. Furthermore, he does not want to be committed to pay for the goods until he has received them. The seller, on the other hand, wants to ensure that once he has dispatched the goods to the buyer, he will be paid by the buyer. The seller would like to receive payment directly into his account at his local bank and in the local currency. Although a seller may request payment for the goods prior to shipment, the buyer is unlikely to agree to such terms. On the other hand, the buyer would prefer to pay for the goods 30 or 60 days after he has received them – but the seller is unlikely to agree, particularly if there is no established trading relationship between the buyer and seller. A solution which satisfies the wishes of both buyer and seller could be to arrange for payment of the goods by letter of credit, otherwise known as a documentary credit.

A letter of credit is a document issued by the buyer's bank on behalf of its customer, the buyer, whereby it agrees to pay funds, in accordance with a draft, to the seller, provided that certain terms and conditions stipulated in the letter of credit are met. The reason a letter of credit is known as a documentary credit is because payment is made solely on presentation of documents, irrespective of the performance of the underlying transaction. For example, if the goods shipped were of the wrong colour or quality (and if this requirement was not to be certified before payment could be made) payment would be made under the letter of credit and recourse of the buyer against the seller would lie under the contract of purchase.

Letters of credit and the methods by which they operate are often confusing to the layperson because they contain 'banking terminology'. The following is a description of the key terms used in a letter of credit:

- *Buyer or applicant* The person or company purchasing the goods and who applies to his bank to issue the letter of credit in favour of the seller.
- *Seller or beneficiary* The person or company selling the goods and who receives payment under the letter of credit.
- *Issuing bank* The bank issuing the letter of credit on behalf of its customer, the buyer or applicant.
- *Advising bank* The bank which is requested by the issuing bank to advise the issuing bank whether the documents required under the letter of credit are in order. If the documents are in order, the issuing bank initiates payment.
- *Confirming bank* The bank which is requested by the issuing bank to confirm to the issuing bank that the documents required under the letter of credit are in order. Unlike the advising bank, if the documents are in order the confirming bank initiates payment to the beneficiary and is reimbursed by the issuing bank.
- *Draft or bill of exchange* The document requiring payment to be made.
- *Documents* The documents specified in the letter of credit which must be presented in order to initiate payment.

The operation of a letter of credit can most clearly be understood by applying a working example. Let us suppose that Seller is a company based in Birmingham, England, which manufactures household water filters in various colours and sizes which can easily be attached to the taps in kitchen sink units. Seller banks with the National Bank of Birmingham which has numerous branches in England, but not in the USA.

Seller believes its water filters will sell well in the USA and has entered into a sales contract with Buyer, a Chicago-based company which sells household plumbing supplies with distribution outlets throughout the USA. The terms of the sales contract between Buyer and Seller provide that Buyer will purchase from Seller 500 water filters and specifies the colour and size. Payment will be made by letter of credit in an amount of £20,000. Buyer's bank is State Bank of Chicago, which has no branches in England.

Having signed the sales contract, Buyer instructs State Bank of Chicago (the issuing bank) to prepare and issue a letter of credit in favour of Seller, as beneficiary, in Birmingham. As State Bank of Chicago has no offices in England, it requests Village Bank of Birmingham (a bank in Birmingham, England) to act as its advising (or confirming) bank. The advising bank will then inform Seller's bank that the letter of credit has been issued.

Seller receives the letter of credit and checks the required terms and conditions against the sales contract. Seller notes that certain documents are required to be presented to the advising bank under the letter of credit, in order to prove that the goods have been shipped and thereby initiate payment. These documents are as follows:

1   Draft in the amount of £20,000.
2   Commercial invoice on the letterhead of Seller giving date of issue, invoice number, description of the goods, price, quantity, port of shipment and name of vessel.
3   Insurance certificate for the goods and shipment to Buyer's warehouse.
4   Certificate of origin showing the country of manufacture.
5   Bill of lading, to be signed by the master of the vessel, which names the vessel and indicates that the goods have been loaded.
6   An inspection certificate signed by an independent third party confirming that the goods meet the quality and quantity specified in the sales contract (normally used for the shipment of commodities, e.g. crude oil, sugar).

Seller notes everything is in order and ships the 500 water filters to Buyer in Chicago. The documents are sent by National Bank of Birmingham to Village Bank of Birmingham (the advising bank) with a copy to State Bank of Chicago (the issuing bank).

The advising bank inspects the documents and if they are all in order will pay (if a confirming bank) Seller and advise the issuing bank, State Bank of Chicago. The issuing bank then examines the documents and reimburses the confirming bank or advising bank if it has paid out under the documents.

The documents are then released by State Bank of Chicago to its customer, Buyer, and the bank receives payment from Buyer (or debits Buyer's account at the bank).

Payment by letter of credit removes the risk of delivery and payment to both the buyer and seller, particularly in international transactions, where the letter of credit is internationally recognized, and is the most popular method of paying for the international sale of goods.

Apart from fraud on the documents, it is almost impossible to prevent payment under a letter of credit. An injunction would be required before a bank would fail to pay under a letter of credit (assuming the documents were in order). Even then, courts are reluctant to grant injunctions under a letter of credit, and very clear proof of fraud is required.

It is therefore important to ensure that the underlying sales contract is very clear with regard to the rights and obligations of the parties regarding the products to be shipped, because the only recourse either party has (assuming the documents are in order and without fraud) is based on breach of contract. Because the entire payment mechanism under a letter of credit is based on documents alone, without consideration of the underlying transaction, it is essential that the documents specified in the letter of credit are clear and unambiguous so as to avoid the possibility of confusion and wrong or non-payment.

Illustrative examples of the trade documents referred to are set out in Chapter 9, and the contents of a letter of credit are set out in Appendix 7.

Transportation terms

Irrespective of how the purchase of goods is financed, it is very important to decide whether the seller or the buyer of the goods carries the risk in the event that the goods are lost, destroyed or damaged in transit. For example, if a container on board a ship leaks and the contents are damaged, who is the responsible party? Likewise, who would be responsible if the lorry carrying the goods has an accident two miles after leaving the manufacturer's factory? Or if, while loading a container on to the ship, the container falls and destroys the contents?

The contract between the parties should stipulate clearly the party responsible for the risk of loss or damage to the goods. This contract can be a formal contract of carriage, can be included as a clause in the sales contract between the parties, or may even constitute a single paragraph on the back of a sales invoice.

Rather than elaborate in specific detail on who is responsible for the risk of loss or damage to the goods in transit, the International Chamber of Commerce has issued an internationally recognized set of terms of carriage which, if incorporated into a contract, designates the party responsible for risk of loss or damage to the goods in transit. These terms are known as Incoterms and are a compilation of the most commonly used terms of carriage around the world. Moreover, Incoterms have specific definitions and have been applied uniformly, thereby avoiding inconsistencies in the interpretation of these terms. For example, the term 'CIF' – cost, insurance and freight – is used under both Incoterms and the US Uniform Commercial Code, but the terms are interpreted differently under the UCC. It is therefore essential to stipulate in the contract or sales invoice whether Incoterms, the UCC or any other trade usage will apply in interpreting the terms of carriage.

There are two further points of which anyone involved with European/US trade should be aware: first, shipping terms have nothing to do with the obligation or time of payment for the goods; and second, it is usual in the UK and Europe for the seller to retain title in the goods pending payment by the buyer. In the USA this is not the case, although in certain cases a filing can be made under the Uniform Commercial Code authorizing the seller to register and notify third parties of its interest in goods.

Although there are over 15 major trade terms for the carriage of goods, the following are the most frequently used terms in a contract for the shipment of goods:

Ex works
A typical 'ex works' clause would read as follows:

Seller shall deliver the goods to buyer ex works, seller's manufacturing facility at Teddington, Middlesex, England.

Under this provision, the seller is obligated to have the goods, in conformity with the contract, ready at its manufacturing facility at Teddington for collection by the buyer at the agreed date. Upon collection, the risk of loss or damage to the goods passes to the buyer, who must insure the goods and arrange for transportation of the goods from the seller's Teddington manufacturing facility. Under an 'ex works' contract, there are minimum obligations upon the seller and maximum obligations upon the buyer regarding risk or loss or damage to the goods.

A point which is often overlooked on an ex works delivery is that the collection-point must be stated. The ex works collection point in the above example is the manufacturer's facility at Teddington.

FOB – free on board
Note that FOB is not an acronym for 'freight on board' – a frequent mistake. A typical FOB clause is as follows:

Seller shall deliver the goods to buyer FOB the port of Hull, England.

Under an FOB delivery, the seller is obligated to deliver the goods to the named port and place the goods on the designated vessel at the specified date. The seller incurs all the costs of transportation of the goods to the port and loading on to the vessel. The seller must insure the goods for transportation to the port. Risk of loss is transferred from seller to buyer when the goods pass over the ship's rail. Thereafter the responsibility for loss and damage to the goods, shipping and transportation at the port of destination is the buyer's.

FCA – *free carrier*

Delivery FCA is similar to FOB, but as FOB is only applicable to ocean transport, FCA can be used for air, road and rail transport and, increasingly, ocean shipment utilizing roll-on/roll-off facilities.

An example of an FCA clause is as follows:

Seller shall deliver goods to buyer FCA Heathrow Airport, London.

The seller's obligation is to place the goods in the hands of the carrier, normally an airline or transport company or railway. The seller must clear the goods for export and insure the goods up to that point. Thereafter the buyer is obliged to insure the goods and arrange for their transport at the destination point.

CIF – *cost, insurance and freight*

A CIF clause will typically stipulate:

Seller shall deliver goods to buyer CIF port of New York, New York.

From a buyer's viewpoint, this is the most favourable delivery clause, as it obliges the seller to pay all the transport and insurance costs, and thereby carry the risk of loss or damage to the goods, until delivery to the buyer at the port of destination when the goods are off-loaded. Under a CIF contract, it is important for the buyer to liaise closely with the seller to ensure that the buyer is satisfied with the seller's level of insurance obtained, as the seller is generally only legally obliged to obtain minimum cover for the goods (a contract under which the buyer is responsible for the insurance is CFR – cost and freight).

Both buyers and sellers should note that the shipment terms will have a significant effect on their pricing policies. For example, a seller's price of his goods will be less on an ex works or FOB basis than they would be on a CIF basis. It is therefore important to clarify the shipping terms in order to avoid unforeseen additional costs when a buyer is negotiating the purchase price of goods.

Tax implications of the investment

Any European company considering the factors influencing its decision to trade with the USA should have an overview of the US tax system, both corporate and individual.

There is both a federal and state tax regime in the USA. While the federal system imposes federal, i.e., US-wide, tax rates, each state imposes its own tax rates. This varies from zero state income tax in certain states to 12 per cent in others. The result of this dual tax regime requires two income tax returns to be completed. However, state and local income taxes are to varying degrees deductible on the federal income tax return. Individual tax returns for taxpayers in the calendar year must be filed by 15 April of the year following the close of the tax year for which the return is being filed.

Unlike many European countries, both corporations and individuals subject to US income tax must file a completed, signed tax return every year. Corporations and self-employed individuals must pay estimated income tax in quarterly instalments.

Corporate income tax
US corporations are taxed on their worldwide income at the following rates (which include marginal rate adjustments):

Taxable income between	Rate
$0 to 50,000	15%
$50,001 to 75,000	25%
$75,001 to 10 million	34%
Over $10 million	35%

In addition, in certain circumstances, corporations may be subject to a 20 per cent Alternative Minimum Tax on their income.

Foreign (non-US) corporations doing business in the USA
A non-US corporation doing business in the USA is taxed on its income relating to the business at the above corporate income tax rates.

The USA has entered into tax treaties with most European countries and with many others, so in all likelihood you will be able to take advantage of the treaty provisions. For example, US tax law imposes a withholding tax on the outward repatriation of dividends, interest and royalty payments from the USA. In the absence of a treaty agreement, the standard withholding rate is 30 per cent. However, under the US/UK tax treaty, the withholding rates for repatriation of dividends to a parent company or another party is 5 per cent and 15 per cent respectively, with zero withholding on interest and intellectual property royalty payments. By contrast, these rates also apply for Germany, but, for example under the US/Spain treaty, the withholding rates are 10 per cent and 15 per cent for dividend distributions to a parent or another party respectively, and 10 per cent withholding on both interest and intellectual property royalty payments.

Additionally, US branches of foreign corporations are also taxed on their worldwide income derived from their US operation.

Individual income tax
US citizens and resident aliens pay federal income tax on their worldwide income, irrespective of where they live. However, US citizens and resident aliens living outside the USA for a full tax year may exclude up to $70,000 of foreign (non-US) earned income.

The income tax rates for individuals depend upon whether the tax return is filed for a single individual or married individuals filing a joint return. For example, for a married couple filing jointly, the 1996 tax rate rises from 15 per cent on taxable income up to $40,100 to a maximum of 39.6 per cent on taxable income over $263,750. The corresponding tax rates for an individual filing a single return are 15 per cent on taxable income up to $24,000 to a maximum of 39.6 per cent on taxable income over $263,750.

Individuals may also be subject to an Alternative Minimum Tax which is assessed at 26 per cent of an individual's first $175,000 of AMT income over the exemption amounts of $33,750 for a single filer, and $45,000 for a joint married filer, and then 28 per cent on AMT income over that amount.

Individual capital gains
The maximum rate on capital gains is 28 per cent.

Miscellaneous taxes

Sales tax   The USA does not generally impose value added tax or sales tax on a federal basis (with the exception of petrol, alcohol and tobacco). However, most states impose a sales tax on goods sold within the state which can be as high as 11 per cent. These taxes are paid by the consumer/customer of the goods at the time of purchase.

Social security tax   A social security system is in force in the USA which provides retirement benefits. The rate depends upon whether a person is an employee or self-employed.

For an employee the employer and employee each pay 7.65 per cent of the individual's first $60,600 of gross income. The rate for self-employed individuals is 15.3 per cent.

A Medicare tax for an employee is assessed at a rate of 1.45 per cent on the employer and employee equally on all wages, and at a rate of 2.9 per cent for self-employed individuals.

A federal unemployment tax is paid by the employer on the first $7000 of the employee's wages at a rate of 6.2 per cent.

11 Immigration and Employment

Immigration

Since its inception in 1798 with the passing of the Alien and Sedition Acts (which permitted the President to deport anyone whom he deemed to be dangerous or a threat to national security and peace), US immigration legislation has endeavoured to maintain a balance between, on the one hand, the constitutional requirement that there is no distinction between citizens and non-citizens and, on the other hand, to control the influx of visitors, citizens and non-citizens into the USA every day. Immigration law has also tended to reflect current-day policy and attitudes of the Congress towards illegal and legal aliens. For example, the border between the USA and Mexico has long been a source of illegal immigrants. While on the one hand these Mexican immigrants provide a hard-working and very cheap labour force, nevertheless they are a drain on the US medical and social service facilities and, the opponents argue, take work which would otherwise be available to legal immigrants or US citizens.

Any person not a national or citizen of the USA must be

given a non-immigrant (temporary) or immigrant (permanent) visa or status by the US government in order to be permitted to enter and/or to remain in the USA for any period of time. The foreign national's activities in the USA are also strictly limited by the type of visa or status acquired. Some visas provide for a wide range of personal and business activities, while others permit little more than short vacation or business visits.

Visa status in the USA is never automatically conferred. Even if a person has made a substantial investment in the USA, has the necessary professional, business or technical skills, has a specific offered job or close family ties, he or she must make an individual application for a particular kind of visa in strict compliance with a very complicated statutory and regulatory scheme for controlling immigration, the most important of which is the Immigration and Nationality Act, and must be granted individual approval of his or her visa or status.

The need for planning

A most important consideration for foreign businesses and investors is the lack of consistency and co-ordination between US tax and corporate laws on the one hand, and US immigration law on the other. A failure to consider applicable tax and corporate law provisions and policies when planning a business move can result in drastically increased US or foreign tax liability. Similarly, a failure to consider long- and short-range personnel considerations and the impact of US immigration law restrictions on the movement of foreign nationals into the USA when planning business moves can result in the failure to bring a key foreign employee or owner into the USA to manage a substantial business or investment.

Differences between immigrant and non-immigrant visas

The essential differences between immigrant and non-immigrant visas concern the duration of the various visas and the scope of permissible activities under each visa category. An immigrant visa has an indefinite duration and permits the holder to engage in the full range of business and personal activities. It typically covers the principal visa applicant and his or her spouse and unmarried children under 21 years of age. All immigrant visa holders may work without restriction in the USA. The only potential disadvantages to immigrant visas or permanent resident status relate to US tax liability on world-wide income and delays in securing an immigrant visa or permanent resident status. Delays for people seeking immigrant visas or a permanent resident status on the basis of business or professional classification can range from three to four months to more than two years, depending upon the category of visa, the place of application, the educational and professional background of the visa applicant, the nature of the position to be held in the USA, and a variety of other factors.

There are numerous categories and subcategories of non-immigrant US visas, several of which may be possible for any one visa applicant. The choice of an appropriate visa category is governed by both immediate and long-range business plans. For example, the choice of a non-immigrant visa category may be dictated by the nature of the job to be taken in the USA, the level of education of the applicant, the nationality of the visa applicant, the possibility that the visa applicant may want to remain in the USA indefinitely, the amount of international travel required by the visa applicant, the age of the children of the visa applicant, the need or desire to have the spouse of the visa applicant work in the USA, the nationality of the owners of the US business, the ownership and management ties between the US business and any foreign affiliated companies or individuals, the size and nature of the US business, or the need or desire of the visa applicant to have his or her children attend school in the USA. The presence or absence of all or some of the foregoing factors in a particular case will dictate the appropriate non-immigrant visa or sequence of non-immigrant visas.

In addition to the factors listed above, the need for speedy issue of a non-immigrant visa must also be considered in the selection of the initial non-immigrant visa. Some non-immigrant visas can be issued within one day by application made directly to a US consular post abroad, while other non-immigrant visas require the previous filing and adjudication of a non-immigrant visa petition with the Immigration and Naturalization Service in the USA.

Although there are 54 categories of non-immigrant visas, the following are the categories most likely to be of interest to investors and business people visiting the USA.

Visitors to the USA for business and pleasure – B-1 or B-2 visa

This category of visa is appropriate for a person who is resident in another country but who wishes to visit the USA for business purposes (B-1) or pleasure (B-2), and who will not be working or earning money in the USA.

Application for either category of visa should be made to a US consulate or embassy abroad. The applicant must show that he or she is resident in and has close ties with the home country (e.g., job, family ties).

Even if a B category visa is granted by a US consulate or embassy overseas, this does not necessarily grant the holder an automatic right of entry into the USA, this discretion being held by the immigration officer at the point of entry. If visiting for business purposes, you are advised to have a letter from your employer stating the nature of the business to be transacted and the length of stay. If entering the country for pleasure, the holder of the visa should have hotel information and a return air ticket, together with adequate funds to support him or her during the holiday. Generally, a holder of a B category visa will be given up to six months in the USA, although it can be extended provided there are valid reasons for the extension request.

The visa waiver pilot program

Nationals of certain countries do not require visas to enter the USA under this scheme, and most European countries, including the UK, fall within it. However, if you travel to the USA frequently, it is still recommended that you obtain a B category visa.

The treaty trader and investor visa – E-1 and E-2 category

This category of visa is available to an individual who is entitled to enter the USA as a result of a treaty of commerce and navigation between the USA and the individual's home country (which includes the UK and most European countries), and who wishes to carry on substantial trade or make an investment in the USA.

Treaty trader

In order to be eligible for a treaty trader visa, the individual must be engaged in the exchange, purchase, or sale of goods and/or services. The trade must also be principally (over 50 per cent) between the USA and the individual's country of nationality, which in turn was party to the treaty with the USA.

Treaty investors

An E-2 treaty investor wishes to enter the USA 'solely to develop and direct the operations of an enterprise in which he has invested, or of an enterprise in which he is actively in the process of investing a substantial amount of capital'.

The test generally applied by the US immigration authorities as to whether funds are 'invested' is whether such funds are actually committed, and that they will be lost if the business or venture fails.

Additionally, the individual must be in the process of investing in a real business, not a paper venture or entity. Although there is no specific dollar amount that should be invested, it is generally accepted that a figure of over $100,000 would be needed to qualify, although a figure of $50,000 has been sufficient. The immigration authorities, however, do apply a test whereby the amount invested should be assessed against the value of the specific enterprise invested in or the amount of investment generally required for an enterprise of that nature.

Intracompany transferee – L-1 category

The general requirement for eligibility for an L-1 visa is that the individual has been employed for at least one year by a company (or other legal entity) and who wishes to enter the USA to provide the same services to his current employer.

The L-1 visa is not, however, available to any employee who satisfies the above criteria. The employee must hold a managerial or executive position or have specialized knowledge.

In order to qualify as holding a managerial position, the individual must (a) manage the organization or a department or division; (b) supervise the work and conduct of other supervisory or managerial employees or manage an essential operation within the organization; (c) have authority to hire and fire; (d) exercise discretion over the day-to-day operations of the organization.

If the individual falls within the category of executive capacity, his activities should include (a) directing the management of the organization; (b) establishing the goals and policies of the organization; (c) have discretion in decision-making policies; (d) may receive general supervision from the board of directors, shareholders, etc.

In order to be eligible for the L-1 visa as a result of having 'specialized knowledge', the individual should possess special knowledge concerning his employer's product, service, research, equipment, techniques, management, its application in international markets, or an advanced level of knowledge or expertise in the organization's process or procedures.

As a general rule, the immigration authorities have applied the criteria for L-1 visa eligibility very restrictively.

Permanent residence

Unlike entrance into the US by visa, the granting of permanent residence in the country carries with it the right to lawfully reside and to live and work there. Upon being granted permanent residence, the individual will be issued a 'green card' which is a plastic card displaying a photograph, fingerprint and other infomation pertaining to the individual.

Applicants seeking permanent residence must either apply for an immigrant visa at a US consulate or embassy overseas, or apply to the US immigration authorities for an 'adjustment of status' if the applicant is already in the USA on a temporary visa.

In order to obtain permanent residence, the applicant must generally either have very close relatives who are US citizens or permanent residents, or have a special skill which is in short supply in the USA. Alternatively, the individual may be able to apply for the 'immigration lottery' where a number of applicants for permanent residence are selected at random or fall within certain quota levels which the US immigration authorities have for certain nationalities.

Permanent residence visas based upon employment skills fall within a quota of 140,000 visas, broken down as follows: 40,000 visas for priority workers which constitute applicants with extraordinary ability in the sciences, arts, education, business or athletics, outstanding professors and researchers and multilingual executives and managers; 40,000 visas for professionals with advanced degrees or exceptional ability in the sciences, arts or business; 40,000 visas for skilled workers, professionals and unskilled labour; 10,000 visas for 'special immigrants', for example religious workers other than ministers; and 10,000 visas for investors who create employment and have an investment of between $500,000 and $1 million, depending upon whether the business is located in a rural or metropolitan area.

The granting of permanent residence carries with it tax repercussions, the most significant of which is that the individual will be subject to US tax on his or her worldwide income.

Employment

The employee/employer relationship in the USA is governed by a combination of state and federal legislation. Compared to many of the European Union countries it is much easier to dismiss an employee in the USA. However, the country has complex legislation addressing equal opportunity and anti-discriminatory rights of employees. Many of the labour cases instituted in the courts revolve around discriminatory practices conducted by employers in the hiring and firing processes.

Before addressing those issues of employment law which are most pertinent to foreign investors in the USA, a distinction should be drawn between union and non-union employees. Union employees are protected by federal legislation and union collective bargaining agreements. The position of unionized employees is outside the scope of this chapter, and the following addresses non-union employees.

Three important areas of employment law are dealt with in this chapter, as they are particularly important for foreign investors doing business in the USA: (a) the employment relationship; (b) the interview/recruitment process; (c) the employment contract.

The employment relationship

The specific employment relationship is governed by state law. However, many states follow the 'employment-at-will' doctrine whereby an employment relationship is terminable at the will of either party and without notice or valid reason. Unlike the UK, a vast number of employees in the USA, from junior level to management, are employed at will and can, and often are, dismissed without notice and with immediate effect.

However, the courts have upheld wrongful discharge cases under two theories – the public policy exception and the implied contract exception.

The public policy exception

This covers instances where an employer dismisses an employee on grounds which undermine public policy – for example, where an employer instructs an employee to commit perjury or be fined, or where an employer dismisses an employee for serving on a jury.

The implied contract exception

This is a more frequent exception to the employment-at-will doctrine, and often an employer finds that an implied contract has inadvertently been created between the employer and the employee.

The implied contract can occur in many situations, but often there is a specific representation made by a company representative regarding the employment relationship – for example, that the employee would only be dismissed for 'just cause'. In many instances, a company personnel manual will have a representation regarding the employee relationship – for example, that no employee will be dismissed without having the opportunity to appear before a committee or will be paid a number of weeks' compensation for every year worked. Employers frequently insert such language in a personnel manual in the interests of maintaining good employee relationships, but do not realize they could be implying a contractual relationship. A contractual relationship has also been implied where an employee has re-located at the request of the employer and has then been summarily dismissed. The courts in this situation have estopped the employer from dismissing the employee.

Myriad legislation covers the employment relationship and includes the Fair Labor Standards Act covering minimum wage requirements, equal pay and record-keeping; the Civil Rights Act which enforces non-discrimination practices in employment on the bases of race, colour, religion, sex and national origin; the Occupational Safety and Health Act which addresses noise levels, air quality and safety equipment. Workers' compensation claims are covered by state legislation which requires workers to be monetarily compensated for losses due to accidental on-the-job injuries.

The employment contract

As the employment-at-will doctrine is so predominant in the USA, it is advisable for employers to enter into contractual relationships with their employees. These can range from a very simple letter of agreement to a formal executive service agreement for senior executives. These contractual agreements should address issues specific to the level and activities of the employee, and at the very least provide parameters for the working relationship. The employment contract should include the following provisions.

Position and duties   The position should be clear and the duties of the employee should be specified. The working hours should be stated and the employee should be required to devote all his or her business time to the job at hand.

Term   Normally for a specific term, automatically renewable for additional terms, unless terminated, or for an unspecified term, until terminated by either party in accordance with the termination provisions.

Compensation   The salary and when payable (weekly, fortnightly or monthly) should be stated. Any deductions (e.g. pension plan, medical and national insurance) should be specified, as should any withholding amounts for tax purposes. If a bonus, discretionary or to be based on performance levels (e.g. commission on sales) is to be given, the time of bonus distribution should be clear. For more senior employees, eligibility for any fringe benefit (e.g. car, travel allowance, expense account, private medical coverage) should be listed.

Performance review   The contract should provide how frequently the employee's performance will be reviewed and by whom.

Vacation   The employee's holiday and vacation settlement should be stated. It is noticeable that holiday entitlements in the USA are significantly less than those for employees in Europe.

Proprietary rights   In today's computerized business environment it is becoming increasingly important for even the most junior employee to agree that the employer has exclusive ownership of all information relating to or useful to the employer's business, including trade secrets, confidential information, customer information, and all intellectual property rights, computerized software programs, and data. These rights are exclusive to the employer, and the employee should undertake not to utilize or retain any such information at the termination of the employment relationship and should return all such property to the employer.

Confidentiality   The employee should agree to keep all information relating to the company confidential upon termination of employment.

Non-competition   Depending upon the seniority and expertise of the employee, an employer may wish to include a non-competitive provision in the contract. However, such a provision should be reasonable and be limited both geographically and in business activity. Generally, courts will protect an employee's right to seek employment and earn a livelihood, and will construe non-compete provisions strictly in favour of the employee and against the employer.

Disability   Any disability entitlement should be stated.

Termination and benefits upon termination   The termination mechanism should be carefully drafted and must be very clear. As an example, the agreement could be terminated upon 30 days' written notice by either party to the other. However, the employee may be able to terminate the relationship immediately for 'good reason', if, for example, the employer required the employee to relocate or seriously demoted the employee. Likewise, the employer could terminate the employee immediately for 'just cause', to include, for example, insubordination, fraud, breach of the agreement.

   Benefits which the employee may receive upon termination should be listed and may include salary for a period of time, medical benefits and possibly the continuation of certain fringe benefits for a period of time.

Notice   The means by which notice to each party should take, such as telefax, courier, registered post, should be clear.

Dispute resolution   In the event of a dispute regarding the employment relationship or the employment contract, the agreement should provide whether the dispute will be resolved through the courts or by arbitration. Juries often hear employment disputes, and their propensity to make high monetary awards make many employers prefer arbitration, the procedure for which should be clearly specified.

The interview/recruitment process

Equal Employment Opportunity (EEO) laws at the state and federal level, as well as affirmative action regulations, have a significant impact on the way each employer recruits and hires. The laws are written to protect specific groups of employees from discrimination: African-Americans, Hispanics, Orientals, American Indians, women, persons over age 40, handicapped persons and US veterans of the Vietnam war. These laws and regulations shape and influence the job qualifications that employers establish, the recruitment sources used, where employers place and how they phrase job advertisements, the questions asked in an interview, the wording of application forms, and the tests utilized, if any, in the applicant-screening process. Compliance with these laws and regulations requires that hiring and recruitment procedures be consistent, uniform and free of any implication of discrimination. The following are important considerations for an employer embarking on the recruitment process.

Recruitment sources

Word-of-mouth recruiting, or using recruitment sources that reach only predominantly white candidates, has been held to be unlawful when the employer has an existing racial imbalance in the workforce. Similarly, preferential hiring of friends, relatives, or personal acquaintances of present employees has been found to be unlawful where the workforce includes disproportionately low minority or female representation.

Qualifications

Job requirements in terms of education, experience or physical characteristics have been found to be unlawful where the requirements tend to screen out or disqualify a disproportionately high percentage of legally protected candidates and they are not justified by any business purpose or requirement in order to perform the basic duties of the job.

This is the 'discriminatory impact' theory of discrimination. An employer can violate the law even where there is no intentional discrimination if the *effect* of the employer's conduct is discriminatory. Under this theory, an enquiry is unlawful if, for example, it requires that applicants for a janitorial position have a high school diploma because (a) the requirement screened out a disproportionate percentage of minority candidates and (b) the requirement was not necessary for effective job performance as a janitor.

Pre-employment enquiries

As a general rule, state and federal EEO laws prohibit the use of all pre-employment enquiries which tend to disproportionately screen out members of minority groups or members of one sex and which are not justified by some business purpose. The position of EEO enforcement agencies is that the information obtained and requested through the pre-employment process should be used solely to assist in the selection of employees based upon qualifications without regard to such irrelevant criteria as race, sex, national origin, age and religion. Accordingly, enquiries which tend to reveal data which bears no relationship to the qualifications for the job sought have been consistently construed as evidence of a discriminatory intent.

Unacceptable pre-employment enquiries

The following pre-employment enquiries are generally regarded as either unlawful or of questionable validity when asked in the *pre*-employment (interview) context.

Applicant's complexion or colour of skin, or race.
Applicant's religious denomination or affiliation.

Whether the applicant is pregnant.

Nature of the applicant's military discharge.

Birthplace of the applicant or applicant's parents, spouse or other close relatives.

How the applicant acquired the ability to read, write or speak a foreign language.

Name and address of a relative to be notified in case of an emergency.

Applicant's arrest record.

Maiden name of the applicant's wife.

Applicant's period of residence in state or city.

Height and weight.

Applicant's marital status.

Number and age of preschool children.

Colour of hair/colour of eyes.

Relatives employed by the company and/or who referred the applicant.

Applicant's military experience in the US armed forces.

Organizations, clubs, societies or lodges of which the applicant is a member, where the name or character of the organization indicates the racial or ethnic origin of its members.

Acceptable pre-employment enquiries

The following questions are legally permissible and may prove helpful as a means of obtaining job-related information about the applicant:

Work experience

How did you originally get your job with your current or previous employer?

Will you describe your present responsibilities and duties?

Describe how you spend a typical day on the job.

What do you consider to have been your major accomplishments at that company?

What are some of the setbacks and disappointments you experienced, or things that turned out less than well? Describe them.

In what way has your job changed since you originally joined the company?

What were your reasons for leaving your previous employers?

How would you describe your present (past) supervisors? What do you consider to have been his/her major strengths and limitations?

In the past, for what efforts have your superiors complimented you? For what have they criticized you?

How do you think your present (past) superior would describe you?

What were some of the aspects about your job that you found most difficult to do?

What were some of the problems you encountered on your job and how did you solve these problems?

What were some of the instances in which you and your superior disagreed?

In what way has your present job prepared you for greater responsibilities?

What is your impression of your present (former) company?

How long have you been looking for another position? What type of position are you seeking?

As you see it, what would be some advantages to you of joining our company?

In what way does the job with our company meet your career goals and objectives?

If you joined our organization, where do you think you could make your best contributions? Why?

Looking into the future, what changes and developments do you anticipate in your particular field?

If you joined our company, what development do you feel you would need to make your best contribution?

Education

Why did you choose the particular college you attended?

How would you describe your academic achievements?

How did you decide to become an (accountant, engineer) etc.?

In what type of extracurricular activities did you participate?

How did you spend your summers while in school?

Have you had any additional training or education since graduating from school?

What were your vocational plans at the time of college (high school) graduation?

How do you think your schooling contributed to your overall development?

What courses did you take which you feel prepared you for the position we have to offer.

Personal factors

In general, how would you describe yourself?

What do you regard to be some of your shortcomings and developmental needs?

What do you regard to be your outstanding qualities?

In which areas do you feel you would like to develop yourself?

What traits or qualities do you most admire in someone who is your immediate superior?

What has contributed to your career success up to the present time?

How might you further your own business career?

What are your long-term goals and objectives?

If you had to do it all over again, what changes would you make in your life and career?

In considering joining a company, what are some of the factors that you take into account?

What other aspects of a job are important to you?

What would you want in your next job that you are not getting now?

What kind of position would you like to hold in five years? In ten years?

What are your present salary expectations? How have you arrived at this figure?

What are your current recreational and leisure time
  interests?
Do you presently belong to any civic or professional clubs
  or organizations? Which ones? Why did you join them?
Do you hold office in any of these? Which office?
How do you spend your vacations?
If you had more time, are there any activities in which you
  would like to participate? Which ones? Why?

Explanation of legal status of specific pre-employment enquiries

There are direct legal implications which may arise as a result
of enquiries concerning the following subjects.

Military record On the basis that minorities receive more
general and undesirable discharges than non-minorities and
that there is no demonstrable relationship between receipt of a
dishonourable discharge and ability to perform the job, the
Equal Employment Opportunity Commission (EEOC) has held
that an employer violates Title VII by requiring job applicants
to produce proof of honourable discharge.

Financial status In the absence of any business necessity
requiring employees to be good credit risks, it is unlawful to
refuse to hire an applicant who has a poor credit status because
minorities tend to have poorer credit records and a lower socio-
economic status generally.

Arrests A request for information concerning arrests tends to
discourage minority applicants and is, therefore, unlawful. Additionally, many state employment discrimination laws specifically prohibit discrimination on the basis of arrest records.

Birth dates Since an applicant's age is not relevant to a consideration of that individual's qualifications for the job, this
question should be avoided. However, an applicant's age can
legitimately be obtained as part of the *post*-employment procedure in connection with the initiation of insurance and

pension plan coverage. Asking an applicant's legal age for child labour law purposes, particularly for employment in 'hazardous' occupations, is also relevant and the following enquiry may therefore be substituted for the birth date question: 'Are you over 18 years of age?'

Height and weight   The EEOC and the federal courts have consistently held that minimum height and weight requirements are presumptively unlawful because they tend to screen out a disproportionate number of minority group individuals and females.

Marital status and dependents   Questions about marital status and number and ages of children are frequently used to discriminate against women and may be in violation of Title VII if used to deny or limit the employment opportunities of female applicants.

Physical defects   Section 504 of the Vocational Rehabilitation Act provides that no 'otherwise qualified' handicapped individual may be excluded from participation in, be denied the benefits of, or be subjected to discrimination under any programme or activity receiving federal financial assistance. This provision applies to employers who contract with the federal government and is applicable to the employment practices of that federal contractor. Department of Labor regulations issued under section 504 with regard to pre-employment enquiries prohibit an employer from enquiring as to whether the applicant is handicapped or as to the nature or severity of a handicap. An employer, however, is permitted to make pre-employment enquiries into an applicant's ability to perform job-related functions.

Additionally, the majority of state EEO laws prohibit discrimination on the basis of handicap which is unrelated to the ability to perform.

Birthplace/citizenship   Enquiries regarding the birthplace of the applicant, or the applicant's spouse, parents or other relatives are generally prohibited. Enquiries regarding the foreign citizenship of the applicant or any enquiry into whether the applicant's spouse or parents are naturalized or native-born US citizens and the date when such person acquired citizenship are similarly prohibited unless a clear job-related reason exists to support the enquiry.

The Immigration Reform and Control Act requires employers to verify the identity and eligibility for employment in the USA of all employees hired after 6 November 1986 and to complete the appropriate verification document (Form I–9). Because of potential claims of alienage discrimination, enquiries necessary for compliance with this law are preferably made *after* the decision to hire has been made. However, applicants may be informed of the legal requirements through inclusion of the following statement on the employment application: 'In compliance with federal law, all persons hired will be required to (1) verify identity and eligibility to work in the USA and (2) complete the required verification document upon hire.'

National origin   Pre-employment enquiries regarding the applicant's nationality, lineage, national origin, descent or parentage, or enquiry about the language commonly used by the applicant, applicant's spouse or parents, are generally prohibited.

Examples of prohibited enquiries include questions such as the following.

> What is your mother (native) tongue?
> What language does your mother speak?
> Were you born in this country?
> Do you have people in the 'old country'?
> That's an unusual name. What nationality is it?

Sex, marital status and family   Enquiry regarding an applicant's sex (unless it is a *bona fide* occupational qualification considered essential to a particular position or occupation), marital status, pregnancy, medical history of pregnancy, future child-bearing plans, number and/or ages of children or dependants, provisions for child care, abortions, birth control, ability to reproduce, and name or address of relative, spouse or children of adult applicant are generally viewed as non-job related and therefore unlawful.

Religion   Enquiry into an applicant's religious beliefs, denomination, affiliation, church, parish, or religious corporation, association, educational institution or society or religious day observance is prohibited.
   Examples of suspect questions are as follows.

> Provide a pastor's recommendation or reference.
>   Does your religion prevent you from working weekends or holidays?
> Do you attend religious services or a house of worship?
> What church do you attend?
> Are you active in any church groups?
> Do you attend church regularly?
> Do you miss work to attend services on religious holidays?

Organizations   A requirement that the applicant list *all* organizations, clubs, societies and lodges to which he or she may belong or enquiries into the names of organizations to which the applicant belongs, including unions and trade or professional organizations, is prohibited if such information would indicate the applicant's race, sex, national origin, handicap status, age, religion, colour or ancestry. On the other hand, enquiries regarding professional associations and memberships are acceptable.

Economic status   Enquiry into an applicant's current or past assets, liabilities or credit rating, including bankruptcy or garnishment, refusal or cancellation of bonding, car ownership, rental or ownership of a house, length of residence at an address, charge accounts, furniture ownership, or bank accounts should be avoided unless they indicate that such information is related to the particular job in question, since they tend to impact more adversely on minorities and females.

Political affiliation   An employer should not request knowledge of an applicant's political affiliation or membership in lawful political organizations which might indicate race, sex, religion, colour, national origin, or country of ancestry, unless a business necessity can be shown.

12 Anti-trust, Securities, Corporation and Environmental Law

Three main areas of federal law influence the activities of companies doing business in the USA. With the exception of the federal tax laws (see Chapter 10), the anti-trust and securities laws, together with federal environmental laws, are an area in which all companies operating in the USA should have at least a working knowledge or they can inadvertently violate a well-established and complicated body of legal commercial practice, with possibly serious repercussions. In addition, the state governed corporation laws are also relevant to the extent that they affect a foreign company's operations in the USA.

Anti-trust law

The USA has one of the oldest and strictest anti-trust (cartel) laws in the world. Unlike the anti-trust laws of the European Union, US law provides for jail terms and substantial criminal fines for a narrow range of offences, such as price-fixing and market sharing, as well as private 'treble' damages suits.

US anti-trust law developed in the late 1800s and early 1900s with the passage of what are today still the four leading pieces of US anti-trust legislation, namely the Sherman Act (1890), which prohibits both unreasonable restraints of competition between competitors (horizontal restraints) and in the chain of distribution (vertical restraints), as well as prohibiting monopolization, attempts to monopolize and conspiracies to monopolize; the Clayton Act (1914), which supplements the Sherman Act and prohibits anti-competitive acquisitions and mergers; the Robinson–Patman Act (1936), which prohibits certain forms of price discrimination; and the Federal Trade Commission Act (1914), which created a commission with regulatory authority to control, oversee and enforce a wide range of deceptive and unfair business practices.

US anti-trust law is based on the premise that monopolies operate to the detriment of the consumer. More recently the anti-trust enforcement agencies and the courts have focused on 'consumer welfare' as the focal point in interpreting and applying the anti-trust laws. In other words, the US anti-trust laws should be applied to preserve competition in order to give consumers competitive prices and to assure consumer choice.

The Sherman Act
Section 1 of the Sherman Act prohibits every form of contract, combination in the form of trust or otherwise, or conspiracy, which may restrain trade or commerce among the states or with foreign nations.

In order for there to be an illegal arrangement, three elements must be present: (a) a tacit or binding agreement; (b) a restraint of competition; and (c) an effect on commerce within the USA or with foreign countries. In 1982 the Sherman Act was amended to remove purely export-oriented restraints from its jurisdiction. Thus, US firms may enter into restrictive agreements whose anti-competitive effects are felt solely *outside* the USA. However, foreign-based anti-competitive activities which have a 'direct, substantial or reasonably foreseeable' effect on US import or domestic commerce are clearly subject to the prohibitions of the Act.

Over the years the courts have given meaning to the Sherman

Act by prohibiting only restraints that 'unreasonably' restrict competition. This is referred to as the 'rule of reason', which requires an evaluation of the purpose and effect of the restraint. As a general rule, restraints imposed by a non-dominant manufacturer on its distributors with respect to customers to be served or territories within which goods are to be distributed are considered reasonable. However, there are other types of restraint, such as resale price maintenance, which are *per se* prohibited.

'Per se' unlawful restraints

The courts have determined that certain categories of restraints are so inherently likely to be anti-competitive that they must be flatly and absolutely prohibited. Accordingly, these types of restraints (so-called *per se* violations) may not be justified by proof that they have no anti-competitive effects under the rule of reason evaluation described above. The principal categories of *per se* violations are price-fixing, bid-rigging, division of markets among competitors or potential competitors, resale price maintenance, certain group boycotts, and certain tying arrangements.

Foreign companies doing business in the USA should carefully avoid each of these categories of restraint. The substantial risks of fines, potential jail terms and private treble damages make it particularly important to avoid mistakenly engaging in these types of activities.

Distribution restraints
Customer and territorial restrictions
As a general rule, it is permissible for a producer or wholesaler whose market share is below 25–30 per cent to appoint an exclusive dealer within a particular territory or a dealer assigned to serve specific classes of customers and not others, provided that the market share of the supplier and the distributor is not high.

Resale price maintenance
It is a *per se* anti-trust violation for a supplier of a product to sell the product to any purchaser on condition that the product be resold at a specified minimum or maximum price.

Policing prices/cutting off discount resellers
Two of the most frequent causes for anti-trust litigation arise when a manufacturer terminates a contract with a dealer. In the first case, a manufacturer may cut off the dealer because the dealer is selling the product at 'discount' prices. By cutting off the low-price dealer, it may appear that the manufacturer is attempting to make an example of the dealer so as to enforce an illegal resale price maintenance policy among all dealers. Because of the *per se* rule against resale price maintenance, it is not permissible for the manufacturer to threaten the dealer or to terminate the dealer relationship in retaliation for selling at 'discount' prices.

In the second case, a manufacturer may cut off a dealer as a result of complaints from other dealers, such as price-cutting, sales to unauthorized territories or customers and so on. In this case, the terminated dealer will allege that the manufacturer and the complaining dealer have engaged in a conspiracy to terminate his dealership.

In both cases it is important that the manufacturer acts strictly on a *unilateral* basis. The manufacturer must not, therefore, give assurances to other dealers or consult with other dealers about how he will handle the troublesome dealer, and must also not indicate that he will continue the relationship with the dealer if the dealer agrees to maintain certain minimum prices.

Section 2 of the Sherman Act makes it illegal to monopolize, attempt to monopolize or conspire to monopolize interstate commerce or trade between foreign nations.

Actions under section 2 have been concluded successfully for actual monopolies, through which a company obtains or preserves a monopoly position (usually involving a market share of at least 50–60 per cent) as a result of competitive practices. Attempted monopolization and predatory pricing where a company may attempt to monopolize a market by setting unreasonably low prices in order to obtain a monopolistic position have become increasingly difficult to establish in recent years.

The Clayton Act

The Clayton Act, at section 3, addresses tying and exclusive dealing activities involving 'commodities'. Section 3 makes it an offence to 'lease or sell goods, wares, merchandise, machinery, supplies or other commodities' on the condition that the purchaser or lessee refrains from dealing with the seller's or lessor's competitors 'where the effect of such lease or sale may be to substantially lessen competition'.

A foreign company investing in the USA should be aware that an exclusive dealing arrangement can be challenged under either the Clayton Act or the Sherman Act.

An exclusive dealing arrangement is one in which a seller agrees to sell its production of a commodity to a specific buyer or where a purchaser of a commodity agrees to purchase its requirements exclusively from a specific seller.

Exclusive dealing relationships are not, however, deemed to be illegal but are viewed under a number of guidelines set down by the courts, such as whether there is a specific product line identified; the geographic market identified; and whether the competition excluded from the arrangement constitutes a substantial share of the appropriate market.

The Robinson–Patman Act (section 2 of the Clayton Act)

Section 2 of the Clayton Act (also known as the Robinson–Patman Act provisions) contains some of the most complex provisions of US anti-trust laws. Section 2 covers discriminatory pricing activities, rebates, brokerage payments, and discriminatory promotional services, in addition to imposing liability upon the buyer for receipt of unlawful discriminatory prices.

The Robinson–Patman Act is of particular importance to companies entering into distribution relationships as the act makes it unlawful to engage in price discrimination between competing purchasers of similar goods where the effect is to substantially lessen competition or create a monopoly. The act does, however, permit discriminatory pricing in order to meet in good faith (but not beat) a lower price offered by a competitor and where there is cost justification.

Section 7 of the Clayton Act

This section of the Clayton Act prohibits any merger or acquisition, whether stock or asset, the effect of which may be 'substantially to lessen' competition, or to tend to create a monopoly.

The provisions of section 7 have been interpreted to include horizontal mergers, which are mergers between companies selling competing goods or services in the same geographic region; to some vertical mergers, which are mergers between companies involved in the chain of supply of goods to customers (for example, between a manufacturer and its distributor), and a very few 'extension mergers' which involve mergers the result of which is to either expand a company's product line or geographical market.

The acquisition or joint venture need not lead to the establishment or strengthening of a dominant position; only a determination that competition is likely to be lessened substantially as a result of the transaction is required. Mergers and joint ventures between companies selling competing goods or services are most commonly challenged by the government anti-trust agencies. However, private suits may also be filed by any person or company which suffers 'anti-trust injury' as a result of the acquisition or joint venture.

The Department of Justice has issued complex guidelines to explain its enforcement policy. As a general rule, mergers and joint ventures between competitors or potential competitors are the most likely to be opposed. The Justice Department pays particular attention to the extent of market 'concentration' and the market shares of the merging firms to make this determination. For example, in a so-called 'moderately concentrated' market with ten firms of equal size (a 10 per cent market share for each firm), the department would be likely to challenge a merger of any two of them. If the ten firms in the relevant market have differing market shares, the department has indicated the following thresholds at which they would be likely to investigate and possibly challenge the merger: combining market shares of 25% and 2%, 16% and 3%, 12% and 4%, 10% and 5%, 8% and 6%, and 7% and 7%. The department is much less likely to challenge other types of mergers, such as 'vertical' mergers (say between a supplier and its distributor) or 'conglomerate' mergers (for example, between non-competitors with no buy–sell relationships, such as between an automobile manufacturer and an airplane manufacturer).

Hart–Scott–Rodino pre-merger notification

A company contemplating a merger or acquisition of a company in the USA should be aware of the pre-merger notification requirements of the Hart–Scott–Rodino Anti-trust Improvements Act of 1976.

Specific pre-printed pre-merger notification forms must be filed with the Federal Trade Commission and the Department of Justice. There is then a 30-day 'waiting period' before the transaction can be completed. This period can also be extended if one of these federal agencies issues a so-called 'second request' for documents or other information, which marks the start of a formal investigation of the transaction.

The basic requirements of the Hart–Scott–Rodino filings are that the acquisition is of voting stock or assets; the buyer or seller is engaged in interstate commerce; that one party has assets or net sales of at least $100 million and the other of at least $10 million; and as a result of the acquisition the buyer will hold at least 15 per cent of the seller's assets or stock or more than $15 million worth of the seller's assets and securities.

Exempt from the Hart–Scott–Rodino notification are real estate or purchase of goods conducted in the ordinary course of business; acquisition of non-voting securities; and the purchase of securities 'solely for investment' or by banks and investment companies and acquisitions where the buyer already holds a 50 per cent voting control of the acquired company and acquisitions approved by federal agencies.

Patents and licensing

The grant of a patent may confer substantial market power on the patentee. The anti-trust laws are intended to permit the patentee to exploit the patent right, but only within the parameters of the patent itself. Over the years, a list of suspect practices has developed that are frequently considered unlawful under the anti-trust laws. Some of the same practices also constitute 'patent misuse', a doctrine of US patent law. The consequence of engaging in a misuse is that the courts will withhold any remedy for infringement or breach of a licence agreement, even against an infringer who is not harmed by the abusive practice. The rights of the patentee will be restored only when the misuse is purged. Purging occurs only when all abusive practices have been abandoned and their harmful consequences have dissipated.

These suspect practices include: (a) tie-ins – requiring the licensee to purchase unwanted materials from the licensor; (b) tie-outs – restricting the licensee's freedom to deal in products or services that are not within the scope of the patent; (c) resale price maintenance – requiring a licensee to adhere to any specified minimum or maximum price relating to the sale of the licensed product; (d) veto power over further licences – agreeing with the licensee not to grant further licences to any other person without the licensor's consent; (e) mandatory package licensing – coercively requiring the licensee to accept a licence under patents in which he has no interest; (f) sales restrictions on product of a patented process – restricting the licensee's sales of products that are made under a patented process; (g) restrictions on purchasers – attempting to restrict a second sale of a patented product, since the patent right is 'exhausted' on the first sale; (h) no contest clauses – an agreement by the licensee not to contest the validity of the patent during the term of the licence; and (i) exclusive grant-backs – requiring as a condition for the licence that the licensee assign back to the patentee any new patent issued to the licensee that is related to the licensed technology.

Very similar principles apply to licences of know-how, trade secrets and trade marks.

The Department of Justice issued guidelines pertaining to the licensing of technology in 1995. These guidelines (which do not have the force of law) suggest that the courts should consider intellectual property on the same basis as any other type of property, that market power should not be 'presumed' to exist just because a patent, trade mark, copyright or confidential know-how are associated with a particular product or service, and that restrictive licensing practices that are not *per se* unlawful in regard to technology that is incorporated into 20 per cent or less of the relevant competing products or services should be considered in a 'safety zone' and therefore presumed as lawful.

Penalties

The US anti-trust laws are enforced by the Anti-trust Division of the Department of Justice, the Federal Trade Commission (FTC) and by private parties who suffer anti-trust injury.

The Department of Justice expends most of its resources against price-fixing and territorial allocations between competitors, bid-rigging, and other restraints of competition between actual or potential competitors. Severe fines and even jail terms are sought when the evidence is clear that the violators knew or should have known that the conduct in which they were engaged was unlawful. Maximum fines are $10 million per offence for corporations and $350,000 for individuals, who are also subject to a maximum of three years' imprisonment per offence. These criminal penalties are most frequently sought for price-fixing and bid-rigging.

The FTC does not have authority to impose criminal sanctions. Instead, it usually seeks equitable relief to terminate or prevent anti-competitive conduct under a special statute, section 5 of the FTC Act. The FTC may also issue orders to prohibit unfair methods of competition, such as deceptive advertising, product mislabelling or deceptive warranties. The FTC also has extensive rule-making authority. For instance, it has issued comprehensive disclosure requirements governing franchises, telemarketing and interstate land sales, and has issued regulations concerning the safety of consumer products.

Finally, natural and juridical persons may sue privately to recover three times the injury that they suffer as a direct result of an anti-trust violation. Direct purchasers who are forced to pay inflated prices for goods which are the subject of price-fixing may, for instance, recover three times the difference between the competitive price and the inflated price. They may also recover their attorney's reasonable fees and costs. In some cases, the treble damages have amounted to many millions of dollars. In recent years it has been particularly popular for a group of private plaintiffs who are similarly situated (such as who all paid inflated prices for a product as a result of a price-fixing conspiracy) to group their claims together in a single action known as a 'class action'.

Securities laws

The sale, purchase and transfer of stocks, shares, bonds, options, investment contracts, investment instruments and financial instruments are highly regulated under the US securities laws, which exist at both the federal and state level.

The federal Securities Act of 1933 and the Securities Exchange Act of 1934 are the two major pieces of legislation regulating the issuance or sale of securities to the public.

In addition to the federal laws most states regulate the issuance and exchange of securities in their respective jurisdictions pursuant to the 'Blue Sky' laws. These Blue Sky laws may apply even if the exchange, issuance or transfer of securities is exempt from disclosure requirements under the federal securities laws. While most states adopt the federal approach and require full disclosure of the risks involved in offering securities, some states also review the merits of the offering and may withhold permission to offer or sell the securities if they deem the offering unfair, deceptive or fraudulent to the public.

Although the provisions of the 1933 and 1934 Acts and the corresponding regulations are complicated, nevertheless, companies investing in the USA should be aware of the more salient features of each of the Acts, particularly if the foreign investor is contemplating acquiring the shares in a US company or marketing investment materials to the US public. Although these requirements can be onerous, nevertheless they do provide public materials which give detailed information on publicly traded companies, for example through the quarterly and annual reporting requirements of the Securities Exchange Act.

The Securities Act

This Act provides a very broad definition of the term 'security' to include any note, stock, treasury stock, bond, debenture, evidence of indebtedness, certificate of interest or participation in any profit-sharing agreement, collateral-trust certificate, pre-organization certificate or subscription transferable share, investment contract, voting trust certificate, certificate of deposit for a security, or, in general, any interest or instrument commonly known as a 'security' or any certificate of interest or participation in, certificate for, receipt for, guarantee of, or warrant or right to subscribe to or purchase, any of the foregoing.

The Act requires securities to be registered with the Securities Exchange Commission (SEC) by filing a registration certificate, unless the security is exempt under the Act.

Section 5 of the Act makes it unlawful to use means or instruments of transportation or communication in interstate commerce or the mail to sell a security through a prospectus or other medium. However, again there is an exemption for certain transactions, which include transactions not involving a public offering.

The Securities Exchange Act

This Act regulates transactions in securities both through securities exchanges and over-the-counter markets. The Act makes it unlawful to manipulate the markets or adopt deceptive practices in the exchange of securities.

Issuers of securities to which the Act applies, and whose sale or exchange involves interstate commerce and use of the mail, are required to register the security by filing a registration statement with the SEC.

An important provision relates to the periodic filing of reports and financial information. With respect to a publicly traded company to which the provisions of the Act apply, of particular relevance are the requirements to file quarterly and annual reports (the 10-Q and 10-K reports) with the SEC. These reports provide very detailed information on the company and its operation. Because the reports are publicly available they often provide a better source of material and information on a company than the formal annual report.

The 10-K report must be filed with the SEC within 90 days of the end of the company's fiscal year and consists of four sections providing specific details on (a) information regarding business issues and activities of the company, real estate and properties owned by the company and major legal proceedings by or against the company; (b) essential information on the company, such as stock exchange price of stock, three years' audited financial statements and management's analysis of the company's financial condition; (c) proxy disclosure information relating to the directors and senior executives, which includes compensation information and beneficial ownership of securities; and (d) requirements for financial statement schedules.

An interesting provision is that the SEC's Electronic Data Gathering Analysis and Retrieval System (EDGAR) enables companies and 'issuers' under the securities laws to file electronically the various information required under the Acts.

Penalties
Anti-fraud and other provisions in the Acts provide the investor, the Securities Exchange Commission and, at the state level, the Secretary of State's office, a right of action against companies and/or individuals who do not comply with the requirements of the acts. Individuals or companies infringing the provisions of the laws face penalties of up to $1 million and, in the case of individuals, five or more years imprisonment.

State 'Blue Sky' laws
Although the state securities laws often contain similar provisions to the federal securities laws, nevertheless, from an

enforcement perspective, the Secretary of State's office in a state will investigate very vigorously violations of the state securities laws which occurred in that particular state. For example, there have been numerous instances of the Secretary of State's office investigating fraudulent practices by investors and which have resulted in a prosecution by the Attorney-General's office in the respective states.

Corporation law

It is often a surprise to foreign companies contemplating investment in the USA that there is no federal corporate law. Corporation law is governed solely by state law, each of which has its own corporate law statute. A foreign company incorporating in the USA must therefore decide in which state it will incorporate.

Although each state's corporation law is similar in many respects to other states' corporation laws, some of the differences can be relevant to a company in deciding in which state to incorporate. Although the general tendency is for a company to incorporate in the state in which it will be doing business, many companies incorporate in, for example, Delaware, even though their principal place of business may be in another state.

There are significant advantages to incorporation in Delaware. For example, that state has a well-established body of legal precedent addressing many issues which arise regarding corporate operations, from directors' fiduciary duties to the rights of minority shareholders. Delaware is also generally regarded as a state which will provide protection to corporations through its laws and has a reputation as being 'pro management'. Additionally, Delaware encourages the incorporation of companies in that state by permitting certain filings to be made by telefax and corporate enquiries and searches to be handled by telephone.

The requirements of the various states' corporate laws are similar to that in the UK. For example, a corporation with limited liability limits the personal liability of the shareholders for the corporation's debts and other obligations of the company. The company is a separate legal entity to the individual shareholders. Forming a company also protects the shareholders from tortious liability of the company.

In many cases a foreign company operating in the USA may wish to form a wholly owned subsidiary there, as it will generally protect the parent company overseas from liability to third parties regarding the conduct of the subsidiary. Without the subsidiary company, the parent company would be liable for obligations it incurred in the USA, including tortious liability, particularly if the product marketed or manufactured in the USA through the US subsidiary brings with it potential product liability exposure.

The concept of an 'off-the-shelf' company does not exist in the USA as it does in the UK. However, in most states it is possible to form a company within 48 hours. The information required will include the names of the officers; president (similar to the managing director in a UK company), secretary and treasurer; classification of shares, if any; purposes of the corporation; name of the corporation; initial capital (in most states there are no minimum capital requirements) and issued and authorized shares. Incorporators file the relevant papers and the articles of incorporation with the Secretary of State's office for the state of incorporation, and the Secretary of State's office will issue the certificate of incorporation.

As with a UK company, US companies have articles of incorporation and a memorandum of incorporation. However, the US articles of incorporation are similar to the UK memorandum of incorporation, and the UK articles of incorporation are known as the by-laws in the USA.

Franchise fees

A company can only be incorporated in one state, but if it is doing business in one or more other states, it is required to register as a 'foreign corporation' in these other states by filing the relevant documents and application forms with the Secretary of State's office in each of these states. The 'foreign company' must also pay a franchise fee for operating in that state, and this fee varies from state to state. However, it is generally based on the authorized share capital, the revenues attributable to that state or a combination of these.

The name of the corporation

Because there is no federal corporation law and no federal name registry, it is possible that two companies with the same name could be incorporated in two (or more) states and may be competing with each other. One method of avoiding this situation is to register the name of the company and/or logo under the federal trade mark law. Any third party which attempted to incorporate a company in another state, although permitted to do so under the corporation law, would not be permitted to do so under the federal trade mark law without violating the trade mark of the first-registered company.

Environmental laws

The USA has some of the most complex environmental laws of any country in the world. Most of the US federal environmental laws have developed since the late 1960s. Before then, liability for pollution and environmental hazards lay in common law principles of imposing liability on parties for damage to persons or property, such as nuisance, negligence, trespass and the imposition of strict liability for ultra-hazardous activities.

Since the 1960s, the US Congress has passed comprehensive laws governing air and water pollution, the transportation of hazardous waste, the manufacture and disposal of toxic materials, medical waste, toxic substances, regulation of pesticides, asbestos and rodent control. The most important provisions are dealt with here, each of which carry with them stringent penalties for violation.

The Environmental Protection Agency (EPA) has overall responsibility for the implementation and enforcement of the environmental laws, though many environmental policies are implemented at regional or state levels, and most states have environmental laws which apply statewide. Unfortunately, the implementation of federal and state environmental laws is not always well co-ordinated.

The complicated interplay of federal and state environmental laws can often appear very daunting to a foreign company establishing operations in the USA. However, the following is a brief overview of the main federal environmental laws which are of greatest importance to foreign companies operating in the USA.

The Superfund

The Comprehensive Environment Response, Compensation and Liability Act, otherwise known as CERCLA, or Superfund legislation, imposes liability and responsibility for the clean-up of land sites upon which hazardous waste has been disposed of in the past, often before the current owner has possession of the property. Liability under CERCLA is very broad and places strict joint and several liability for the costs of remediation and cleaning up of a polluted site among four categories of person:

- current owners and operators of the site;
- previous owners and operators of the site who owned or operated the site when the hazardous materials were disposed of;
- the party arranging for the treatment or disposal of the hazardous substance disposed of at the site;
- the persons who transported the hazardous materials to, and selected, the site.

Liability is retroactive, even if a party's involvement with the site was before 1980, the date when the CERCLA legislation was enacted.

Only four defences are available to a potentially liable party under CERCLA, namely that the disposal of the hazardous waste and the resulting damages were caused by (a) an act of God; (b) an act of war; (c) an act or omission of a third party unrelated to the potentially liable party; and (d) that the current owner purchased property, after an appropriate enquiry, which later became a CERCLA site (otherwise known as the 'innocent purchaser defence').

Because of the very limited defences available to potentially liable persons under CERCLA, companies acquiring land in the USA should require stringent representations and warranties from the seller with regard to the environmental condition of the land being purchased; in addition, if possible, they should obtain an indemnity for costs or damages from the seller if environmental liability is later imposed upon the purchaser.

These warranties are particularly important if an otherwise liable person will be relying on the 'innocent purchaser defence'.

Essentially, under this defence, purchasers of property who are potentially liable under CERCLA can possibly avoid liability if they purchased the property without knowledge of the con- tamination after exercising a due diligence enquiry, and mitigated the damage by exercising due care once they realized that the contamination existed and took adequate precautions regarding the person responsible for the contamination.

Partly as a result of those requirements, environmental audits are frequently conducted by a purchaser of land, and companies can, and should, be retained who specialize in conducting environmental audits.

Air pollution

This is governed by the provisions of the Clean Air Act which regulate 'stationary' sources (such as factories, manufacturing facilities) and 'mobile' sources (such as motor vehicles) of air pollution.

National ambient air quality standards are implemented under the Clean Air Act through state procedures which implement air pollutant restriction plans. The Act specifies certain air quality standards which have to be met, and regulates facilities that emit air pollutants above certain threshold levels. The Act also contains a list of hazardous air pollutants.

There are continuing efforts both federally and statewide to improve the quality of the air and reduce pollution. For example, motor vehicles have to meet stringent air pollution emission control tests and, effective from the beginning of 1995, petrol stations have to install vapour-blocking valves on all petrol hoses to reduce benzene vaporization.

Water pollution

Water pollution is governed by the Clean Water Act (the Water Pollution Control Act 1972), and regulates the discharge of water pollutants, irrespective of the quality discharged.

The Clean Water Act authorizes a permit programme for direct discharges of pollutant, treatment standards of pollutants to publicly owned treatment works, the regulation of storm water and accidental discharges of pollutants, and permits programmes for the protection of wetland areas.

Hazardous waste

A significant portion of the environmental laws in the USA addresses the treatment and handling of hazardous waste. The Resource Conservation and Recovery Act (RCRA) regulates all aspects of handling hazardous waste, from its inception and transportation to its use and final disposal.

Hazardous waste has four characteristics – ignitability, corrosivity, reactivity and toxicity. Waste falling above certain threshold levels for each of these criteria must be handled, transported, stored and disposed of within strict requirements of the RCRA. Specific types of waste listed by the EPA as hazardous are also subject to RCRA's requirements.

The RCRA requires a generator of hazardous waste to submit periodic reports to the EPA and state regulatory agencies; provide accurate records regarding the elements of the hazardous waste and treatment of these constituents in the event of a spill; contract only with duly authorized and licensed carriers of hazardous waste and disposal centres; and ensure that appropriate containers with required labels and warnings are used in connection with the hazardous materials. In addition, transportation companies of hazardous waste must meet stringent standards, including being licensed and ensuring that vehicles carry appropriate warning signs and instructions for the treatment of hazardous waste in the event of a spill, and clearly displaying emergency contact numbers on the vehicle.

All hazardous waste is also subject to manifesting before, during and at the end of any journey. Owners and operators of facilities which treat, store or dispose of hazardous waste must obtain RCRA permits and comply with an extensive array of operating and reporting requirements.

13 Dispute Resolution

Irrespective of the routes by which an investment in the USA takes place, whether by an agent/distributor network, a joint venture or formation of a subsidiary company, the issue of how a dispute is resolved is invariably overlooked. In the enthusiasm of investing in the USA the last consideration of the parties is, 'what happens in the event of a dispute', yet when a dispute arises the first provision in any agreement to be evaluated carefully is the dispute resolution clause.

In deciding how a dispute should be resolved, the parties have recourse to either litigation or what is known as ADR – alternative dispute resolution – which includes mediation, the mini-trial and arbitration. There is an increasing trend in the USA for disputes to be resolved outside the court litigation process and to rely on arbitration or mediation. Although the ADR process in Europe is becoming more popular, it lags behind the popularity of ADR in the USA.

Whichever dispute resolution process the parties may adopt, the appropriate clauses should be drafted very carefully and incorporated into the agreement. Examples of dispute resolution clauses applying to litigation, arbitration, the mini-trial and mediation are to be found in Appendix 11.

In deciding whether to adopt litigation or an ADR procedure, the nature of the anticipated dispute is relevant. In a situation where immediate relief may be required, for example a request for an injunction to prevent infringement of a trade mark, immediate access to a court of law is important. It is not therefore unusual to find an arbitration clause in an agreement specifying that any dispute under the agreement will be resolved by arbitration, but reserving the right to apply to a court for an injunction or specific performance in the event that immediate and urgent equitable relief is required.

A consideration of dispute resolution procedure would be incomplete without also addressing the governing law of the dispute resolution process and the aspect of enforcement of a judgment or arbitral award against the opposing party. These two considerations are also analysed below. However, it is important first to understand what is meant by mediation, a mini-trial, arbitration and litigation as a possible dispute resolution mechanism, and the respective merits of each.

Mediation

Mediation is an extension of the negotiation process and is conducted by a third-party mediator, appointed by the parties, who works with the parties in order to resolve the dispute.

Unlike an arbitrator, a mediator does not have the authority to render a binding decision, but conducts joint and individual meetings with the parties in order to identify and understand the issues in dispute and assist the parties in working towards an amicable solution.

A mediator does not hear formal testimony between the parties, nor does he require specific evidence of the issues in dispute. The mediator will, however, attempt to reduce any hostility between the parties and encourage a discussion on areas which one or both parties may have overlooked and areas of strengths and weaknesses of each party's case.

The agreement by the parties to mediate can take place either at the time the contract or agreement was entered into by inserting a mediation clause into the agreement, or by submitting the dispute to mediation at the time the dispute arises. It is advisable in the event of mediation in the USA that the parties conduct the mediation process under the guidance of, for example, Endispute or the American Arbitration Association, which has offices throughout the country.

The appointment of an experienced mediator can greatly facilitate the mediation process. Such a mediator may be a judge, lawyer or other experienced individual, and it is highly recommended that the selected mediator is experienced in the area of the dispute. Various organizations in the USA maintain lists of fully qualified and trained mediators in specific areas of expertise who can be called upon to mediate a dispute.

A mediator's objective is to assist the parties in reaching a workable resolution for the settlement of a dispute. Once this is achieved, the mediator, often assisted by the parties, will reach a written agreement, which is accompanied by releases from either party. In many mediation cases, the settlement agreement is incorporated into a consent award. In cases where mediation fails, the dispute may be submitted to arbitration or litigation, in which event the materials and information obtained during the mediation process cannot be used as evidence unless with the consent of both parties.

The mini-trial

A mini-trial is the procedure by which each party presents its side of the dispute, often through counsel, before business executives and an independent third party who acts as a neutral adviser. Business representatives of each party are present during the hearing. After the submission of both parties' case, the parties meet with the neutral adviser to negotiate a settlement.

One advantage of the mini-trial is that it is private, confidential and non-binding, and yet enables a full exchange of information to take place. Although discovery takes place, the neutral adviser and counsel will generally ensure that discovery is limited to issues which are pertinent and relevant to the dispute. One of the main objectives of the mini-trial is to identify the strengths and weaknesses of each party's case and to establish any common ground upon which settlement negotiations can be initiated.

As a mini-trial is non-binding, either party can withdraw at any time. Moreover, the business executives or neutral adviser hearing the case may be requested to render a written 'judgment' giving their conclusions on the merits of the evidence as to which party would have, in their view, prevailed.

Arbitration

Arbitration is the most popular form of ADR and is increasing in popularity, particularly as a viable alternative to the litigation process.

Arbitration has certain advantages over litigation which can be very important to the respective parties.

1   It ensures the neutrality of the arbitrators and avoids the perception that one party may be subject to an unfriendly or biased court, particularly if a case is being heard in the 'home court' of one of the parties.
2   As the arbitrator, or arbitrators, are selected by the parties (or a nominating body) it enables individuals with experience in the field of the dispute to be selected by the parties. This can be very important where technical issues are involved in the dispute, for example in the patent or computer technology fields.
3   Arbitration provides a flexibility of procedure which is often lacking in litigation. Arbitration hearings do not generally follow the strict rules of evidence, and hearsay evidence is frequently permitted.
4   The parties are guaranteed privacy with regard to the proceedings and the subject matter of the dispute. This is

particularly important where a party deems it essential that there is no publicity surrounding the award or arbitral hearings. This is in sharp contrast to litigation proceedings in the USA, where the pleadings are a matter of public record and television cameras in the courtroom are not uncommon. Moreover, the decision of an arbitral panel is not publicized.

5   Although the cost of arbitration will depend on the specific rules of the arbitral organization supervising the proceedings, the cost is generally less than litigation.

6   International enforceability of an arbitral award is in many cases easier than enforcement of a judgment, due to the 1958 Convention on the Recognition and Enforcement of Foreign Arbitral Awards.

7   The location of both the arbitration hearings and nationality or residence of the arbitrators can be agreed upon by the parties in advance of the hearings. For example, it is not unusual to have international arbitration take place in a neutral venue such as London, Paris, New York or Zurich.

Institutional arbitration

There are a number of institutional arbitration organizations in existence but, for a company or individual involved in a dispute involving a US party, there are three important ones.

The International Chamber of Commerce (ICC)

The Court of Arbitration of the International Chamber of Commerce is one of the leading international arbitration institutions for the settlement of international commercial disputes, although the word 'court' is something of a misnomer because the court's role is essentially to referee arbitration proceedings. Under the ICC rules, the parties are required to address such matters as governing law, selecting the arbitral tribunal and determining the place of arbitration. However, should the parties fail to agree on or implement any of these issues, the Court of Arbitration will intervene.

The Court of Arbitration monitors the conduct of the arbitration and screens requests for arbitration which are referred to the court either directly or through the national committee in the country of the referrer. The request for arbitration contains information such as the names, description and addresses of the parties, the statement of the claimants' case, the supporting documents and relevant particulars concerning each parties' choice of arbitrators. The court then approves the terms of reference prepared by the parties and the arbitrator. The terms of reference clearly define the issues which are the subject-matter of the arbitration; they are signed by both sides and a meeting serves as a pre-trial conference. The court also monitors the arbitration proceedings and resolves any procedural questions which the arbitrators may refer to the court. Finally, the court scrutinizes the award prepared by the arbitrator both as to form and substance. Although the court may modify the arbitrator's award, it must do so without affecting the arbitrator's liberty of decision.

American Arbitration Association (AAA)

The AAA is one of the leading arbitral organizations in the USA, is based in New York and has offices and hearing facilities in over 35 cities. The AAA is unique in that it performs arbitration services for specific disputes. For example, there are specific services available for commercial, construction, patents and computer software disputes.

Unlike ICC arbitration, the AAA adopts a flexible, broadly structured approach to arbitration and provides the arbitrators with considerable discretion in the procedures and conduct of the case. The AAA is also considerably faster and less expensive than ICC proceedings.

A unique feature of the AAA is that the arbitrators are generally not encouraged to render a written opinion giving the legal and factual bases for their decisions. Although the parties are permitted to request such an opinion, the lack of an opinion can be problematic for parties from civil law jurisdictions where jurisprudential public policy requires a reasoned opinion.

An advantage to AAA arbitration is that enforcement of a decision in a US court is relatively easy as the US courts are familiar with the AAA and its procedures. A further advantage is that the AAA assigns a case administrator to each case. The case administrator handles all the correspondence between the arbitrators and the parties and resolves any administrative questions or issues.

Arbitrators under the AAA have complete discretion on how to run the hearings, and a typical first meeting will resolve all administrative and legal issues and set a discovery schedule leading to a hearing date.

The London Court of International Arbitration (LCIA)

The LCIA was inaugurated in 1892 as the London Chamber of Arbitration and is one of the oldest arbitration institutions in the world.

The LCIA is an international organization and is very competent to oversee complex international disputes. The LCIA consists of a president, four vice-presidents and up to 26 other members. Up to six of the members are from the United Kingdom, with the remainder being selected from the major commercial centres of the world.

The international capability of the LCIA is particularly apparent through the LCIA's 'users councils' which cover the major trading regions of the world and consist of four councils covering Europe and the Middle East, North America (including Mexico and Canada), Asia-Pacific (covering South-East Asia and the Pacific Rim) and the Pan-African council (covering the countries of sub-Saharan Africa).

The LCIA acts as the organization appointing arbitrators under the rules of the LCIA and under the arbitration rules adopted by the United National General Assembly on 15 December 1976 (UNCITRAL rules). In addition, the LCIA acts as the appointing authority where an arbitration clause in an agreement requests the LCIA to appoint the arbitrator or arbitrators to hear a dispute. The LCIA also implements the functions conferred upon it by the LCIA rules and the UNCITRAL rules, such as case administration.

Both the LCIA rules and the UNCITRAL rules give the arbitrators considerable autonomy and maximize the jurisdiction and powers of the arbitrators.

'Ad hoc' arbitration

Unlike institutional arbitration, which follows specific guide-lines and rules of arbitration under the supervision of internationally recognized arbitral organizations, *ad hoc* arbitration is managed by the parties according to their own rules. *Ad hoc* arbitration is generally appropriate in very limited circumstances, particularly where a specialized knowledge or expertise is advantageous to the parties, such as disputes concerning oil concession agreements, boundary and territory lines, and commodities futures and derivative markets.

A key factor in ensuring a successful *ad hoc* arbitration is the selection of competent arbitrators with experience not only in the subject-matter of the dispute, but also in arbitration practice and procedure and the rules of evidence.

Litigation

If the parties to an agreement elect not to specify arbitration or mediation to settle a dispute, either party may have recourse to litigation in the US courts.

As mentioned earlier, recourse to the court system is most appropriate in certain cases, for example where immediate relief is required, such as granting an injunction.

However, the US court system can be very daunting for a foreign company operating in the USA. Some of the issues which such a company should be aware of before subjecting themselves to litigation are as follows.

1   There is both a federal and a state court system. One important difference is that state court judges are elected by voters in that state, but federal court judges are approved by the President and the Senate. Although the federal court jurisdictional requirements would in most cases result in a foreign company with a dispute over $75,000 litigating in a federal rather than a state court, nevertheless litigation may be held in a state court if the foreign company operates through a subsidiary company in the USA.

2   Civil cases can be tried before a jury as well as by a judge sitting alone, and juries tend to award the quantum of damages. This can result in excessive damage awards for what are often considered to be frivolous lawsuits. Moreover, punitive and treble damages can be awarded where a defendant's conduct is wilful.
3   The evidential discovery process in the USA includes the taking of depositions from witnesses. This is almost a 'mini-trial' where witnesses are cross-examined by the opposing lawyers. Although one of the purposes of the deposition is to elicit information which may lead to a settlement of the matter before it reaches trial, it can nevertheless make the length of time before a dispute reaches court excessive.
4   There is no rule in the USA that the unsuccessful litigant pays the successful litigant's costs. Litigation can therefore be very expensive, and there is no disincentive regarding costs to dissuade a plaintiff from lodging a frivolous lawsuit. Moreover, a number of attorneys in the USA will accept cases on a contingent fee basis, whereby they take an average of one-third of the award of damages to their client if the client is the successful party; if their client loses, however, they receive no fees.

For these reasons, it is perhaps not surprising that arbitration and mediation are becoming an increasingly popular means of settling disputes.

Enforcement of a judgment or arbitral award

Whether the parties to an agreement consent to have a dispute settled by litigation or arbitration, neither forum is appropriate if a final judgment or arbitral award is not enforceable against the party against whom it is rendered.

In order to examine this situation there are two separate and distinct scenarios which must be considered.

Enforcement of a US judgment or arbitral award in the USA

Judgments of a US court are enforceable in the USA subject to any rights of appeal or legal grounds that one party may have for staying the enforcement process. Moreover, through the 'full faith and credit' provisions of the US Constitution, a judgment of the court of one state is generally enforceable through the courts of another state.

Similarly, arbitral awards of a US arbitral panel are generally enforceable through the US courts (subject to any appeal process which may be open to the parties).

Enforcement of a foreign (non-US) judgment or arbitral award in the USA

This is a more complicated issue and depends upon whether the decision being enforced in the USA is a judgment of a foreign (non-US) court or an arbitral award.

Enforcement of a foreign judgment

Unlike the enforcement of foreign arbitral awards, as described below, there is no formal treaty or convention addressing the multilateral enforceability of foreign judgments.

Enforcement of foreign judgments has been based on the common law doctrine of comity. In summary, the doctrine of comity will permit a foreign judgment to be enforced in the US courts if there has been the opportunity for a full and fair trial in the foreign country, if adequate notice of hearing before a court of competent jurisdiction was given to the parties and, if the hearing was held under a system of jurisprudence which permits its own citizens and citizens of other countries to receive a fair and impartial trial with the issuance of an impartial decision. However, one important consideration in applying the comity doctrine is whether there is reciprocity between the USA and the foreign country whereby judgments of US courts would be enforced in the courts of that foreign country.

Foreign monetary judgments

Where the foreign judgment being enforced in the USA is a monetary judgment, the common law principles of comity have been codified in the Uniform Foreign Money-Judgments Recognition Act, which has been adopted by many US states.

The Act applies to any foreign judgment which is final and conclusive and enforceable where rendered even though an appeal from such judgment is pending or is subject to appeal. A foreign judgment is defined in the Act as any judgment of a foreign state granting or denying recovery of a sum of money, other than a judgment for taxes, a fine or other penalty, or a judgment for support in matrimonial or family matters.

Nevertheless, even if a foreign judgment is 'final', 'conclusive' and 'enforceable where rendered', the foreign judgment need not be recognized (a) if the defendant in the foreign court did not receive notice of the proceedings in sufficient time to prepare a defence; (b) if the judgment was obtained by fraud; (c) if the cause of action was against public policy of the US court; (d) if the judgment conflicts with another final and conclusive judgment; (e) if the proceeding in the foreign court was contrary to an agreement between the parties as to how the dispute was to be settled; or (f) if the foreign court was a seriously inconvenient forum for the trial of the action.

Enforcement of a foreign arbitral award

The 1958 Convention on the Recognition and Enforcement of Foreign Arbitral Awards was the result of attempts by many international organizations to secure the enforcement of arbitral awards between different countries. Both the USA and the UK have ratified the convention, as have most of the developed countries of the world.

The convention applies to the recognition and enforcement of arbitral awards rendered in countries signing the convention. The term 'arbitral award' includes awards made by arbitrators appointed by the parties for each case (*ad hoc* arbitration) and also those awards made by permanent arbitral bodies to which the parties have submitted (such as the AAA or the LCIA).

In order to enforce foreign arbitral awards in the USA, the

enforcing party has to provide an authentic original award, or certified copy, and the original arbitration clause in the agreement or contract which was the subject-matter to be disputed.

The convention does, however, recognize seven grounds for refusing to enforce an arbitral award: (a) that the arbitration agreement was invalid or the parties were under some incapacity under the governing law of the arbitration agreement; (b) the party against whom the award is invoked was not given proper notice of the proceedings or the appointment of the arbitrator; (c) that the award deals with issues not contemplated by or not falling within the arbitration or contains matters outside the scope of the arbitration agreement (although the valid points of the award can be severed from the invalid parts); (d) that there was an irregularity in the composition of the arbitral tribunal; (e) that the award has not yet become binding on the parties or has been set aside or suspended by a competent authority in the country in which the award was rendered; (f) the subject-matter of the dispute is not capable of settlement by arbitration under the laws of that country; or (g) the recognition or enforcement of the award would be contrary to the public policy of the enforcing country.

Governing law

The governing law of an agreement between two foreign parties is often overlooked, with the result that arbitration proceedings or litigation are invariably delayed pending a decision by a court or arbitral panel on the governing law of a contract which is decided after taking into account such issues as where the agreement was signed, where performed, by whom, and a general analysis of the contractual obligations.

These issues can be avoided by stating in the agreement which law will govern the resolution of any dispute between the parties. Although the selected governing law should have some link or nexus to the parties, each party should analyse carefully which governing law is more appropriate for them in the event of a dispute. This is not always obvious.

For example, let us suppose that company E, a UK company, is entering into a contract for the sale of goods with company A, a US company. Company E has no assets in the USA and company A has no assets in the UK. From the viewpoint of company E, the initial reaction as to which law should govern a dispute under the agreement may be to have the contract governed by English law, a jurisdiction in which company E is very familiar. However, company A may object to English law and insist on US state law to govern the agreement, which may actually be advantageous for company E. If US state law governs the agreement and company E brings an action (either arbitration or litigation) against company A and succeeds, company E can immediately enforce the award or judgment against the assets of company A in the USA. Moreover, if company A succeeds, and company E has no assets in the USA, company A has to enforce the arbitral award or judgment in the English courts, and is subject to company E raising issues challenging the enforcement of the award by company A in England.

Appendix 1:
Checklist for a distribution agreement

1. Appointment of distributor and scope of agreement

   a   Exclusive/non-exclusive
   b   Products and services
   c   Territory

2. Duties of distributor

   a   Best efforts/sales promotion (solicit orders, quote prices, use order forms)
   b   Reports (sales calls, orders, prospects, complaints)
   c   Installation service
   d   Maintenance and repair service
   e   No warranties on behalf of manufacturer
   f   Indemnification for unauthorized representation and warranties
   g   Credit checks
   h   Business insurance

3. Duties of manufacturer

   a   To supply the product
   b   Product information
   c   Advertising material

d Technical advice and support
e Notice of price change, product modifications
f Installation and support service
g Warranties

4. Status of distributor and acceptance of orders

a Distributor as independent contractor
b Rights in trade names or trade marks
c Acceptance of orders by manufacturer or distributor
d Cancellation of orders by customers, distributor or manufacturer
e Delivery
f Line of credit/consignment sales
g Appointment of sub-distributors

5. Commission and compensation

a Define price (net price, adjustments, $/£ shifts, taxes, duties)
b Commission as fixed sum/percentage of price
c Other compensation of distributor (bonuses, other incentives)
d Rental or lease equipment
e Split commissions

6. Confidentiality/industrial property rights

a Written materials – return of all copies
b Confidential technical information, know-how
c Confidential business information
d Registration of patents and trade marks

7. Term and termination

a Term, e.g. 1 year, renewable upon written consent of parties
b Notice of termination, e.g. 90 days
c Insolvency, bankruptcy, failure to be ongoing business

d   Change of ownership, assignment
e   Conflicts of interest

8.   Miscellaneous terms

 a   Notices
 b   Assignment
 c   Severability
 d   Waiver of breach
 e   Arbitration
 f   Entire agreement
 g   Governing law
 h   Prior agreements
 i   Amendments
 j   *Force majeure*

Appendix 2:
Checklist for a licence agreement

1. Definitions

    a Licensed technical information
    b Licensed products
    c Net sales, etc.

2. Licence grant

    a Exclusive/non-exclusive
    b Territorial area
    c Manufacture/have manufactured/use/sell
    d Appointment of sub-licensee/sub-contractor
    e Use of trade mark
    f Continuing update on improvements

3. Prosecution and protection of intellectual property

    a Action for infringement by licensor with financial contribution by licensee

4. Sub-licensing and/or sub-contracting

    a Rights confirmed or denied

5. Payments

    a Down payment
    b Running royalties (based on net sales)
    c Minimum royalty payment
    d Royalty-free period during an initial term

6. Accounts

    a Regular provision of accounts to licensor re licensee and any sub-licensee
    b Currency and mode of payment

7. Technical exchange

    a Licensor to licensee for defined period
    b Further developments and improvements passed to licensee
    c Improvements made by licensee

8. Confidential information

    a Obligations of licensee and licensor

9. Warranties of licensor

    a Ownership of rights
    b Power to license rights
    c No outstanding infringement actions
    d No warranty re future patent grant or non-infringement by manufacture/sale

10. Warranties of licensee

    a Non-assignment
    b Best efforts to manufacture/have manufactured/use/sell
    c Recognition by licensee of ownership of intellectual property by licensor

11. Complying with governmental obligations

    a   Responsibility of licensee

12. Indemnity and limitation of liability

    a   Licensee to hold licensor harmless
    b   Limitations on liability of licensor

13. Duration

    a   Term of years
    b   Life of patent rights
    c   Unlimited
    d   Renewability

14. Termination

    a   Royalty payments in arrears
    b   Non-performance of terms
    c   Failure to reach specification
    d   Financial collapse of licensee
    e   Result of termination

15. Consultancy

    a   Appointment of licensor by licensee
    b   Terms of appointment – years, fee, duties

16. Miscellaneous terms

    a   Notices
    b   *Force majeure* provisions
    c   Waiver
    d   Arbitration
    e   Governing law
    f   Assignment
    g   Severability
    h   Entire agreement

Appendix 3:
Typical distributorship agreement

THIS AGREEMENT is entered into this _____ day of _____, 199–, by and between _____, a company with its principal place of business at _____, England, hereinafter called the ('Principal') and _____, a company with its principal place of business at _____, USA, hereinafter called the ('Distributor').

WHEREAS, the Principal manufacturers widgets and wishes to sell, distribute and market such widgets in the Territory (as hereinafter defined).

WHEREAS, the Distributor is an established company experienced in the sale, distribution and marketing of widgets and has a well established and experienced distributor network throughout the Territory.

NOW, THEREFORE, in consideration of the mutual promises herein and other good and valuable consideration, the receipt of which is hereby acknowledged, the parties agree as follows:

DEFINITIONS
'Products' shall mean all widgets listed in Schedule 1 hereof and manufactured by the Principal whose manufacture, use or sale falls within the scope of any claims of the British Patent No. GB _____ and Patent Application PCT No. _____

and any other products which may be added from time to time upon written agreement of the parties.

'Technical Information' shall mean all technical and proprietary information relating to the manufacture, operation, use and sale of the Products.

'Intellectual Property' shall mean the Products more fully described in British Patent No. _____ and in PCT Application No. _____, copies of which are attached (the 'Intellectual Property Patents') and trade marks relating to the Products, copies of which are attached (the 'Intellectual Property Trade Marks').

'Territory' shall mean the states of the USA listed in Schedule 2 hereof

1   **APPOINTMENT OF DISTRIBUTOR**
        The Principal hereby appoints the Distributor an exclusive Distributor for the Territory in respect of the sale and marketing of the Products or any part thereof for an unlimited term commencing on the date of execution of this Agreement. The Distributor will have the exclusive right to purchase the Products or any part thereof from the Principal for resale in the Territory for the duration of this Agreement.

2   **GENERAL UNDERTAKING BY DISTRIBUTOR**
2.1   The Distributor shall during the continuance of this Agreement diligently and faithfully serve the Principal as its Distributor in the Territory and shall use its best endeavours to improve the good will of the Principal in the Territory and to further and increase the sale of the Products in the Territory.

2.2   The Distributor shall not do anything that may prevent the sale or interfere with the development of sales of the Products in the Territory including the sale of any competing products.

2.3   The Distributor will ensure that it conforms with all legislation, rules, regulations, statutory and legal requirements existing in the Territory from time to time in relation to the Products, and is responsible for any contravention of such requirements including infringement of any Intellectual Property rights.

2.4 The Distributor undertakes to store the Products under conditions that will prevent deterioration. The Distributor is responsible for clearing the Products through customs and other import formalities and that pending such clearance the Products are stored as aforesaid. The Distributor agrees to allow the Principal or its authorized representative to inspect the Products when in storage upon reasonable notice.

2.5 The Distributor undertakes not to copy, produce, make, modify or manufacture or assist any other party to copy, produce, make, modify or manufacture the Products or any part thereof for use, sale or any other purpose except as provided under the terms of this Agreement.

2.6 The Distributor shall leave in position and not cover or erase any notices or other marks which the Principal may place on or affix to the Products.

2.7 The Distributor shall send to the Principal an inspection report on each shipment of the Products received by the Distributor as well as such other information on the quality and performance of the Products as may from time to time be reasonably required of the Distributor by the Principal.

2.8 The Distributor undertakes that it will indemnify the Principal against all proceedings, costs, liabilities, injury, loss or damage arising out of the breach, negligence, performance or failure in performance by the Distributor of the terms of this Agreement.

2.9 The Distributor undertakes that it will not purchase the Products or any part thereof from any source other than the Principal or a source duly licensed by the Principal.

2.10 The Distributor undertakes that it will furnish to the Principal any significant development, improvement or advancement relating to the Products and/or the Technical Information which comes to the notice of the Distributor, during the term of this Agreement.

2.11   The Distributor undertakes to take out and pay for the necessary product liability insurance cover for the Products unless it is encompassed by the corresponding insurance of the Principal, in which event the Distributor will pay the agreed proportion of the premium.

2.12   The Distributor undertakes that it will use the Intellectual Property Trade Marks of the Principal, or other mark approved by the Principal, on all the Products and on all packaging, publicity and advertising material used in conjunction with the Products or any part thereof.

2.13   The Distributor undertakes that it will not sell the Products or any part thereof outside the Territory without the written permission of the Principal.

3   **APPOINTMENT OF SUB-DISTRIBUTORS**
The Distributor is permitted to appoint sub-distributors in connection with the sale and marketing of the Products, PROVIDED ALWAYS that the Distributor shall remain responsible for the activities of any such sub-distributors and such appointment of sub-distributors shall only be made with the Principal's written consent.

4   **ENQUIRIES**
The Principal shall during the continuance of this Agreement refer all enquiries received by it for sale of the Products in the Territory to the Distributor. The Distributor shall refer to the Principal all enquiries for Products for sale into areas outside the Territory.

5   **SUPPLY, PRICE AND PAYMENT**
5.1   The Distributor shall purchase all its requirements for the Products ready packaged from the Principal, unless it is agreed in writing by the Principal that the Products or any part thereof shall be purchased by the Distributor in non-packaged form.

5.2   The parties hereto agree that orders for the Product will be placed by the Distributor on a monthly basis and shall be on the terms set out herein.

5.3 The price at which the Products shall be invoiced to the Distributor shall be based upon the currently published export prices of the Principal as shown in its catalogues and other publications, copies of which shall from time to time be supplied to the Distributor by the Principal. Where any price of the Products or of the cost of packing thereof notified to the Distributor is increased, such increase shall not operate until three months has elapsed from the date of receipt by the Distributor of particulars of the increase.

5.3.1 Invoices shall be paid in £ sterling currency to the Principal at its bank in England, by irrevocable confirmed letter of credit for a period of two (2) years from the date of this Agreement and thereafter on credit terms subject to satisfactory credit references and checks.

5.4 The Principal reserves the right to improve or modify the Products without prior notice but the Distributor shall be notified of such improvements or modifications.

5.5 The Distributor recognizes that the Principal shall not be liable to the Distributor in the event that third parties import the Products into the Territory and offer the same for sale therein, provided such importation and offer for sale was carried out without the knowledge or approval of the Principal.

5.6 Each shipment of the Products made by the Principal in response to the Distributor's orders shall be regarded as a separate contract of sale and no one default in a shipment shall be cause for terminating the relationship between the parties hereunder.

5.7 All orders received by the Principal from customers in the Territory shall be referred to the Distributor.

5.8 The Principal shall not sell any Products to third parties outside the Territory which the Principal knows will be sold or placed in the Territory and the Principal will pass such orders to the Distributor.

5.9 Full particulars of the specifications of the Products so far as the Distributor needs to know shall be furnished by the Principal to the Distributor whether for marketing purposes, labelling or the like, and the Principal agrees to provide the Distributor with all information necessary to permit the Distributor to organize a good publicity and sales promotion campaign.

5.10   Orders placed by the Distributor to the Principal shall only be deemed accepted if acknowledged and accepted by the Principal in writing.

5.11   Orders so accepted will be fulfilled as speedily as practicable and shall be shipped FOB port of Hull, England.

5.12   The Principal will at the request of the Distributor pack the Products suitably for delivery to such destination as shall be designated by the Distributor.

5.13   In the event that the Principal supplies Products that do not conform to those specified in the order, and that satisfactory checks have been carried out by the Principal, Distributor or an agent appointed for the purpose, the Principal will take back the Products and will reimburse the Distributor any reasonable expenses incurred.

5.14   The Distributor shall bear any customs duties and taxes that may be levied by reason of importation.

5.15   The Distributor agrees to minimum purchases of the Products in accordance with the following scale:

5.15.1   The date on which minimum purchase requirements operate is the date on which the Distributor receives the first shipment of the Products as manufactured by a commercial process and in a form accepted by the trade as being technically correct, hereinafter referred to as the 'Date'.

5.15.2   During the first year after the Date, the Distributor intends to purchase _____ Products, but failure to do so will not result in termination of this Agreement.

5.15.3   During the second, third, fourth and fifth years after the Date, the Distributor undertakes to purchase _____, _____, _____ and _____ Products respectively. Failure to achieve such purchase targets will result in termination of the Agreement or at the Principal's discretion conversion to non-exclusive distributor.

5.15.4   During subsequent years the Distributor undertakes to purchase not less than _____ Products.

5.15.5   Notwithstanding anything hereinbefore contained the obligation to make minimum purchases of the Products shall, at the absolute discretion of the Principal, be subject to revision by the Principal in the event that the Distributor can show to the satisfaction of the Principal good reason why such minimum purchases cannot be achieved.

6   **DISTRIBUTOR'S RECORDS**
The Distributor shall keep accounts together with supporting vouchers and other relevant papers showing all orders for the supply of the Products by the Principal to the Distributor and by the Distributor to its customers and shall allow the Principal or its authorized representative at all reasonable times to inspect audit and copy the same for the purpose of checking any information given by the Distributor to the Principal or of any other of the obligations to be performed by the Distributor under this Agreement.

7   **ADVERTISING AND MERCHANDISING**

7.1   The Distributor shall notify to and agree with the Principal not later than the end of October in each calendar year an advertising and sales promotion programme for the Products for the next calendar year. This programme may be varied by the Distributor in the light of current market conditions during the course of the relevant year.

7.2   The cost of all initial advertising and sales promotion activities shall unless otherwise decided be borne by the Distributor.

7.3   All advertisement, point of sale, promotion, merchandising and publicity material for the Products issued by the Distributor shall be subject before issue to the prior written approval of the Principal.

7.4   The cost of all merchandising returns from customers

relating to the Products shall (unless otherwise agreed in writing), be borne by the Distributor.

7.5   The Principal hereby authorizes the Distributor to use the Intellectual Property Trade Marks which are the property of the Principal on the Products supplied by the Principal without payment of a fee during the life of this Agreement.

8   **PROSECUTION AND PROTECTION OF INTELLECTUAL PROPERTY**

The Principal shall diligently assist in the prosecution and maintenance of the Intellectual Property and shall diligently take all steps necessary to assist with obtaining, maintaining and extending any letters patent or protection with respect to trade marks and copyright and other intellectual property rights in respect thereof. During the term of this Agreement an intellectual property protection insurance for the term set out therein and thereafter as available from reputable underwriters shall be maintained in force in respect of the Intellectual Property Patents and the Intellectual Property Trade Marks and trade mark applications and copyright falling under the defined Technical Information. A proportion of the cost of such insurance shall be borne by the Distributor, reimbursement to the Principal being effected within twenty-eight (28) days of presentation of the relevant invoice.

In the event that the Distributor learns of any infringement or threatened infringement of any of the Intellectual Property the Distributor shall forthwith notify the Principal. The Principal shall, in conjunction with the Distributor, consider the position. If, in the sole discretion of the Principal, an infringement action is commenced, the Distributor shall provide all reasonable information and assistance to the Principal and all costs associated with such proceedings and those costs incurred by the Distributor in providing such information and assistance to the Principal shall be borne by the Distributor and the costs shall be reimbursed as and when reimbursement of said costs become available from the intellectual property rights insurance underwriters.

9   **TERM OF AGREEMENT**

9.1   This Agreement shall (subject to early termination as herein provided) commence upon the date set out herein and continue in force for an unlimited term.

9.2   The Distributor shall obtain at its own expense all necessary consents and licences (including but without limitation those required to be given by any government department or any body constituted under the law of the Territory for licensing or other regulated purposes relating to the Products) to enable the Distributor to market, distribute and sell the Products in the Territory and obtain any other governmental permission, consent or licence necessary for the full and legal operation of this Agreement.

9.3   The Distributor shall not be entitled to any compensation on the termination of this Agreement.

9.4   In the event that the Principal wishes to sell or otherwise dispose of its business and that an acceptable offer is made to purchase or take control of the business, the Principal will immediately notify the Distributor in writing. The Distributor will then have the right to
      (a)   purchase the business on the same terms as offered to a third party or
      (b)   to join with the Principal on mutually acceptable terms to jointly run the business.

10   **TERMINATION**
      Without prejudice to any right or remedy the parties may have against each other for breach or non-performance of this Agreement, (a) the Distributor shall have the right to terminate this Agreement for breach by the Principal of its undertakings in clause 12 hereof upon the expiration of 30 days' notice to the Principal to rectify such

breach, and (b) the Principal shall have the right summarily to terminate this Agreement:

10.1   On the Distributor committing a breach of any of its obligations including non-payment of any invoice, all of which shall be considered as of the essence, providing the Distributor has been advised in writing of the breach and has not rectified it within thirty (30) days of receipt of such advice.

10.2   If the Distributor shall have any distress or execution levied upon its goods or effects.

10.3   On the commencement of the winding-up or bankruptcy of the Distributor or on the appointment of a receiver of the Distributor's assets or on the Distributor ceasing to do business at any time for sixty (60) consecutive days (other than for annual holidays).

10.4   On the Distributor for any reason of whatsoever nature being substantially prevented from performing or becoming unable to perform its obligations hereunder.

10.5   On the Distributor assigning or attempting to assign this Agreement without the prior written consent of the Principal.

10.6   If control of the Distributor shall pass from the present shareholders or owners or controllers to other persons whom the Principal shall in its absolute discretion regard as unsuitable.

11   **EFFECT OF TERMINATION**

11.1   Upon termination of this Agreement for any cause whatsoever (including but without limitation expiry by effluxion of time), the Distributor shall at the request of the Principal promptly return to the Principal the Technical Information and all documentation of any nature whatsoever in its possession or control relating to the Products (including but not limited to brochures and sales correspondence) or to the Principal and to the activities of the Distributor in relation to the Products or the Principal (other than correspondence between the Distributor and the Principal which does not relate to technical matters).

11.2 Upon such termination the Distributor shall have no further rights to use the Intellectual Property in any way whatsoever and in particular but without prejudice to the generality of the foregoing shall cease to use the Intellectual Property Trade Marks on its letterheads, packaging, or elsewhere.

11.3 Upon such termination the Distributor shall (if so required) supply the Principal with a list of the Distributor's customers for the Products.

11.4 Upon such termination, the Distributor shall (if legally possible) assign to the Principal free of charge all permissions, consents and licences, if any, relating to the marketing and/or distribution and/or sale of the Products and execute all documents and do all things necessary to ensure that the Principal shall enjoy the benefit of said permissions, consents and licences after the said termination to the entire exclusion of the Distributor.

11.5 Upon termination the Distributor shall not sell the Products unless with the express written approval of the Principal to allow the distributor to dispose of existing stock.

12 GENERAL UNDERTAKINGS BY PRINCIPAL

12.1 The Principal warrants that it will not sell the Products or any part thereof into the Territory during the term of this Agreement.

12.2 The Principal warrants that during the term of this Agreement it will not grant a licence to sell the Products or any part thereof into the Territory to any third party.

12.3 The Principal is the sole owner of rights, titles and interests in and to the Technical Information.

12.4 The Principal has the full power and authority to enter into this Agreement and that there are no other agreements, understandings or commitments whether written or oral to which the Principal is a party which in any manner prevent or conflict with the entering into and performing this Agreement.

12.5   No claims for patent infringement, trade mark infringement, copyright and/or design right infringement, restraint of trade, unfair competition, interference with business or contractual relations have been filed or, to the best of its knowledge, threatened, by a third party, against the Principal with respect to any Technical Information or the licence and grant thereof to the Distributor.

12.6   The Principal warrants that the Products will be free of manufacturing defects. NO FURTHER WARRANTIES, WHETHER EXPRESS OR IMPLIED ARE GRANTED.

13   **CONFIDENTIALITY**
The Distributor shall keep strictly confidential, not disclose to any third party and use only for the purposes of this Agreement all information including, but not limited to, the Technical Information relating to the Products whether technical or commercial and to the affairs and business of the Principal and its subsidiary or associated companies, whether such information is disclosed to the Distributor by the Principal or otherwise obtained by the Distributor as a result of its association directly or indirectly with the Principal. Information in the public domain shall not be regarded as confidential.

14   **TRANSMISSION OF RIGHTS**
This Agreement and the benefit of the rights granted to the Distributor by this Agreement shall be personal to the Distributor who shall not without the prior written consent of the Principal assign the same or part with any of its rights or obligations hereunder.

15   **DISPUTES**
Any controversy or claim arising out of or relating to this agreement or the breach, termination or validity thereof, which cannot be settled amicably by the parties, shall be submitted to arbitration in accordance with the [Com-

mercial Arbitration Rules of the American Arbitration Association] before a panel of three arbitrators. Each party shall appoint one arbitrator and the two arbitrators so appointed shall appoint the third. The venue of the arbitration proceedings shall be [New York, New York]. The arbitration proceedings and all pleadings and correspondence relating thereto shall be in the English language. The decision of the arbitration panel shall be final and binding on the parties and judgment on the award rendered by the arbitrators may be entered in any court having appropriate jurisdiction.

16   **SEVERABILITY**
In the event that any one or more of the provisions contained in this Agreement shall for any reason be held to be unenforceable, illegal or otherwise invalid in any respect under the law governing this Agreement or its performance, such unenforceability, illegality or invalidity shall not affect any other provisions of this Agreement and this Agreement shall then be construed as if such unenforceable, illegal or invalid provisions had never been contained herein.

17   **COMPLIANCE WITH LAWS**
In the performance of this Agreement both parties shall comply with all laws, rules, regulations, decrees and other ordinances issued by any governmental or other state authority relating to the subject-matter of this Agreement and the performance by the parties hereto of their obligations hereunder.

18   **FORCE MAJEURE**
Neither party shall be liable to the other for any failure to perform or delay in performance of its obligations hereunder caused by any circumstances beyond its reasonable control, including but not limited to defaults of suppliers or sub-contractors for any reason whatsoever and all types of industrial disputes, lockouts and strikes.

19   **WHOLE AGREEMENT**

19.1   This Agreement sets forth and shall constitute the entire agreement between both the parties with respect to the subject-matter hereof and shall supersede any and all promises, representations, warranties or other statements whether written or oral made by or on behalf of one party to the other of any nature whatsoever or contained in any leaflet, brochure or other document given by one party to the other concerning such subject-matter.

19.2   This Agreement may not be released, discharged, supplemented, interpreted, amended, varied or modified in any manner except by an instrument in writing signed by a duly authorized officer or representative of each of the parties hereto.

20   **NOTICES AND OTHER COMMUNICATIONS**

20.1   Any notice and any permission, consent, licence, approval or other authorization to be served upon or given or communicated to one party hereto by the other (in this clause called a 'Communication') shall be in the form of a document in writing transmitted by facsimile with hard copy by air courier including without limitation a telex, cable or facsimile.

20.2   All Communications shall be made to the Principal and to the Distributor at their addresses as set out earlier in this Agreement.

21   **STAMP DUTY**

The Distributor shall be responsible for the presentation of this Agreement to the relevant fiscal and other authorities of the Territory for the purposes of assessment and stamping in accordance with the laws of the Territory relating to stamp duty upon documents of the same nature as this Agreement. The Distributor shall effect such presentation as soon as possible after the signing hereof and shall be responsible for the timely presentation, stamping and payment of stamp duty in accordance with such laws. The Distributor shall be responsible for the stamp duty or other relevant costs, expenses and disbursements (if any) and also for any penalties payable by reason of failure to comply with time limits for presentation or payment or other requirement laid down by the said laws.

22   **RELATIONSHIP BETWEEN THE PARTIES**
The Distributor and the Principal are independent contractors and neither party is acting as the agent, joint venture partner or is in any manner or form affiliated with the other party.

23   **PROPER LAW**
The construction, performance and validity of this Agreement shall in all respects be governed by the laws of England.

Signed by the duly authorized signatories of the parties hereto.

For and on behalf of the Principal

....
For and on behalf of the Distributor

....

SCHEDULE 1
PRODUCTS

SCHEDULE 2
TERRITORY

Appendix 4:
Typical licence agreement

THIS AGREEMENT is entered into this _____ day of _____, 199–, by and between _____ ('Licensor') a company with its principal place of business at _____, and _____ ('Licensee'), a company with its principal place of business at _____.

WHEREAS, Licensor manufactures widgets and desires to license Licensee to manufacture same in the Licensed Territory.

WHEREAS, Licensee has the relevant expertise and knowledge of the appropriate market and wishes to accept such licence.

NOW, THEREFORE, in consideration of the mutual promises herein and other good and valuable consideration, the receipt of which is hereby acknowledged, the parties agree as follows:

DEFINITIONS
1 'Licensed Products' shall mean widgets used and sold under the 'Licensed Technical Information'.
2 The 'Licensed Territory' shall mean the United States of America.
3 'Licensed Technical Information' shall mean all licensed patents, trade marks, know-how, trade secrets, proprietary information and technical data which are currently owned by Licensor together with all improvements relating to the design, construction or manufacture of widgets.

(a)   'Licensed Patents and Trade Marks' shall mean the patents and trade marks and patent and trade mark applications within the Licensed Territory as set forth in attached Exhibit A [see page 207] including any division, continuation, continuation-in-part or substitute patent and trade mark application.

(b)   'Know-how', 'Trade Secrets', and 'Proprietary Information' shall mean all the technical, experimental and other knowledge, unpatented inventions, manufacturing secrets, secret processes, formulae, manufacturing procedures, representing current accumulated experience which Licensor receives with respect to the licensed rights.

(c)   'Technical Data' shall mean designs and working drawings, plans, specifications, manuals and other similar tangible material with respect to the licensed rights which are currently owned by Licensor.

(d)   'Improvements' shall mean any improvement made during the term of this Agreement and covered by the claims of the Licensed Patents and Trade Marks or any Technical data relating thereto.

GRANT

4(a)   Subject to the terms and conditions of this Agreement, Licensor hereby grants to Licensee the non-exclusive right and licence, without the right to sub-license, to use the Licensed Technical Information to make, use and sell Licensed Products within the Licensed Territory during the term of this Agreement.

(b)   This Agreement shall become effective and binding upon Licensor and Licensee upon the execution by the parties of this Agreement.

ROYALTIES

5   Licensee shall pay to Licensor royalties as follows:

(a)   *Start-up period* This licence shall be royalty-free from the date of execution hereof for a period of two years.

(b)   *Royalties to commence in [year]* Commencing on [date],

Licensee shall pay to Licensor for a period of twelve (12) years a royalty of five per cent (5%) of the net sales price of the Licensed Products.

(c)   As used herein, 'net sales price' shall mean gross sales price of Licensed Products, less any deductions for returns, cost of repair for returned or rejected Licensed Products, discounts, or allowances. All sales shall be deemed to have taken place on the date of invoicing or shipping, whichever last occurs.

6(a)   The royalties due under paragraph 5(b) shall be paid on the basis of calendar quarter instalments and shall be subject to the following:

(i)   Licensee shall provide to Licensor within thirty (30) days after the termination of each calendar quarter a written report setting forth the gross sales price and net sales price of Licensed Products during the preceding calendar quarter, and a computation of the royalty accruing during such period.

(ii)   The report shall be accompanied by a certified cheque payable in [country] to the order of Licensor in the amount shown by such report to be due and payable as a royalty hereunder.

(b)   All royalties owed to Licensor under this Agreement shall be paid to Licensor by Licensee free and clear of all taxes, including excise and governmental fees, and all such taxes shall be borne and paid by Licensee for its own account.

7   Licensee shall maintain at its principal office, and shall cause its affiliates to maintain adequate books of account and records showing its actions under this Agreement. Such books and records shall be open to inspection, during usual business hours and at Licensor's expense, by an independent certified public accountant designated by Licensor, and for two (2) years after the calendar quarter to which the royalties pertain, for the purposes of verifying to Licensor the accuracy of the royalties paid by Licensee under this Agreement.

QUALITY

8   Licensee agrees and undertakes that it is required and its affiliates shall be required to maintain the quality of the Licensed Products in accordance with the standards presently being used by Licensor. In this regard, Licensee shall give Licensor access to manufacturing facilities and shall provide Licensor with representative Licensed Products.

RELATION BETWEEN THE PARTIES

9   It is understood that this Agreement does not establish any relationship between the parties other than that of licensor and licensee and that neither party is hereby constituted the agent, joint venture partner or affiliate of the other.

TECHNICAL ASSISTANCE

10(a)   Licensor agrees to render to Licensee assistance by way of advice, instruction and consultation at Licensor's facilities in [location] at such reasonable times and for such reasonable periods as shall be necessary for the practical utilization and exploitation by Licensee of the Licensed Technical Information. In connection with such assistance Licensor will furnish to Licensee such samples, prints or drawings as it shall have in its possession or as it shall subsequently acquire including those relating to Improvements of the Licensed Products made during the term of this Agreement relating to the manufacture and use of the Products. Licensor will make available at its facilities in the United States of America a qualified technician or technicians or engineer to work with and give such assistance, including its method of production and quality control, to a qualified technician or engineer from Licensee as is necessary for Licensee to properly utilize Licensee's Licensed Technical Information in the manufacture and use of the Licensed Products provided that all travel and living expenses, salaries and fringe benefits of such technician or engineer of Licensee shall be borne by Licensee, and that Licensee pay Licensor a *per diem* of [amount] for each of the

Licensee personnel to whom technical assistance is rendered hereunder.

(b) Upon request of Licensee, Licensor will meet annually with Licensee's technically qualified representatives to review design improvements, new applications, or changes and improvements in the manufacturing methods of the Licensed Products.

(c) Upon request of Licensee and subject to the availability of Licensor's personnel, Licensor shall make available to Licensee at its manufacturing facilities in the United States of America for reasonable periods of time technically qualified personnel to provide technical assistance. Licensee shall reimburse Licensor for all relevant out-of-pocket expenses including round-trip transportation, hotel and meal expenses, and shall pay Licensor a *per diem* of [amount] for each such employee.

CONFIDENTIALITY

11 Any know-how, trade secrets or proprietary information, whether in the form of technical data or otherwise, obtained by either party to this Agreement or to any licence granted hereunder, relating to such Agreement or licence, the rights granted thereunder and the business of the other party, as a result of the relationship between them which is not generally known and available to the public or which was not previously known to the other party, and which is in the nature of information that gives the owner thereof a competitive advantage in the conduct of its business, shall be held in confidence and shall not be disclosed by such party to any other person or entity without the written consent of the other party. Such prohibition shall not apply, however, to disclosure by either party to its employees, affiliated companies, consultants, independent contractors, patent representatives, and attorneys, to the extent reasonably necessary to the performance of this Agreement and the licence or licences granted hereunder; provided, however, that each party shall take all reasonable precautions in a manner acceptable to the other party to ensure

that such know-how, trade secrets, proprietary information, or technical data is not disclosed, reproduced, or used by such persons in contravention of this provision. Unless otherwise provided, the obligation of each party relating to such know-how, technical data, trade secrets, or proprietary information shall survive the termination of this Agreement and the licence or licences granted hereunder.

IMPROVEMENTS

12   Licensor shall provide to Licensee full details and particulars of all improvements relating to Licensed Products which during the term of this Agreement it owns or controls, or may discover, or which may come under its control, whether patented or not, and Licensee shall during the term of this Agreement be entitled to use and benefit thereof without any further payments.

13   Any improvements made by Licensee during the term of this Agreement relating to Licensed Products under this Agreement or relating to the manufacturer of such Licensed Products shall be disclosed to Licensor, and Licensor shall grant to Licensee during the term of this Agreement a royalty-free, paid-up, non-exclusive licence to make, have made, use and sell such improvements for use in the Licensed Products.

PROTECTION OF INTELLECTUAL PROPERTY

14   Licensee expressly acknowledges and agrees that, except in the Licensed Territory and to the extent of the grant set forth in paragraph 4, it does not acquire under this Agreement any rights in or to the use of the Licensed Technical Information or patents used or adopted in connection with the Licensed Products by Licensor anywhere in the world. All Licensed Technical Information furnished to Licensee hereunder remains the property of Licensor.

15   Licensee agrees that it will not at any time contest anywhere in the world ownership of any of the patents, utility model rights, design rights or trade marks of Licensor related to the Licensed Products or Licensed Technical Information,

nor may Licensee contest their validity, except in those countries where Licensee cannot be legally foreclosed by contract from doing so.

16   Licensee agrees that it will promptly notify Licensor of any products being distributed in the Licensed Territory which infringe the Licensed Patents, Licensed Technical Information, designs and inventions of Licensor, and shall take action to stop such infringement in the Licensed Territory.

ASSIGNABILITY

17   This Agreement and the licence granted under it may be assigned (1) by Licensee with substantially all its business related to the subject matter of this Agreement only with the prior written consent of Licensor, or (2) by Licensor to any firm or corporation directly or indirectly controlling, controlled by, or under common control with Licensor. Each party shall promptly advise the other in writing of any such assignment.

DURATION

18   Unless terminated under paragraph 19 hereof, this Agreement shall remain in full force and effect until _____.

TERMINATION

19   This agreement and the licences granted under it may be terminated:

(a)   By mutual agreement of Licensor and Licensee.

(b)   In the event either party shall be in default by failing to observe or fulfil any condition or representation of this Agreement, the other party shall have the right to serve upon such defaulting party a written notice specifying such default, requesting the remedying thereof within ninety (90) days from the date of said notice. If such default is not satisfactorily remedied within said period, the other party may serve the defaulting party with a written notice of immediate termination of this Agreement, upon which all rights and licences, except those which are irrevocable or which may have accrued hereunder at the date of such notice, shall be cancelled, and each party will execute whatever documents may be necessary to return the rights or property of the other parties which may have been acquired hereunder.

(c)   In the event that Licensee or Licensor shall become insolvent, or file a voluntary petition in bankruptcy, or an involuntary petition in bankruptcy shall be filed against Licensee and Licensee shall remain undischarged for a period in excess of ninety (90) days, or Licensee and Licensor shall enter into a compromise with creditors generally, or Licensee and Licensor shall become bankrupt or otherwise lose control of its business involuntarily, or Licensee and Licensor shall be dissolved for any reason, Licensor shall be entitled to terminate this Agreement in its entirety forthwith.

FURTHER AGREEMENTS: CO-OPERATION

20(a)   Licensor and Licensee shall enter into such further agreements as may be required by the laws of any jurisdiction in order to protect their rights under this Agreement and the licences granted hereunder.

(b)   Licensor and Licensee shall co-operate fully in executing all papers and doing all acts necessary to carry this Agreement into effect.

POST-TERMINATION

21(a)   Upon termination of this Agreement, Licensee shall have the right for six (6) months to dispose of all Licensed Products, or substantially completed components, parts, or elements thereof, then on hand which when assembled would constitute such Licensed Products, and to complete all orders for Licensed Products then on hand, and royalties where due shall be paid with respect to such Licensed Products as though this Agreement had not terminated.

(b)   Upon termination of this Agreement, Licensee agrees not to use Licensed Technical Information or improvements disclosed by Licensor to Licensee during the term of this Agreement, for any purpose for a period of ten (10) years from the date of termination. In addition, Licensee agrees promptly to return to Licensor all of the Technical Data and to use reasonable efforts to destroy all copies thereof, except for one copy which may be retained by Licensee for the sole purpose of determining the continuing obligations of Licensee, Licensor, affiliates and related companies under this Agreement.

(c)   Upon termination of this Agreement, Licensee shall prepare a final accounting which shall include all Licensed Products. Licensee shall not withhold any moneys accrued, due and payable by Licensee to Licensor hereunder, on the ground of a dispute arising out of or in relation to this Agreement and as set-off against any claim for damages sought to be put forward by Licensee.

INDEMNIFICATION AND RELEASE

22   Licensee shall indemnify Licensor and hold it harmless against and from any liability, claims or damages and expenses whatsoever in any way arising out of Licensee's negligent manufacture, distribution or use of the Products, and Licensee hereby further releases Licensor from any liability, claims, damages or expenses in any way arising out of Licensee's negligent manufacture, distribution or use of the Products.

23   Licensor hereby agrees to protect, indemnify and hold harmless Licensee for and against liabilities, losses, expenses and damages of any kind whatsoever arising from claims of patent or trade mark infringement asserted by any other person, firm or corporation against Licensee in respect of the importation, distribution, use or sale of the Licensed Products in the Licensed Territory. Licensee shall promptly notify Licensor in writing of any claim or suit by a third party alleging such patent or trade mark

infringement. Licensee shall not, without the knowledge and written consent of Licensor, enter into any correspondence with a third party who has asserted a claim or instituted an action alleging such patent or trade mark infringement, nor shall Licensee do anything which would or could prejudice the defence to such claim or action by such third party. Licensor shall be entitled in the name of Licensee but at its expense to assume the sole conduct and control of the defence of any such claim or action instituted by a third party. Licensee shall render all reasonable assistance in connection with the defence to such proceedings as Licensor may request.

FORCE MAJEURE
24 Neither party shall be liable for failure to perform its part of this Agreement when the failure is due to causes beyond its reasonable control such as, but not limited to, fire, flood, strikes, labour troubles or other industrial disturbances, inevitable accidents, war (declared or undeclared), embargoes, blockades, legal restrictions, riots, insurrections, or governmental regulations.

WAIVER
25 A waiver by either party hereto of any right it may have under this Agreement or by reason of its breach shall not imply the waiver of any other right or a subsequent waiver, nor shall it affect the validity or enforceability of any provision hereof.

SEVERABILITY
26 Should there be a final determination by a competent authority to the effect that one or several of the provisions, or any part thereof, of this Agreement are invalid, the remainder of this Agreement shall continue in full force and effect. In this event the parties shall attempt to agree on new provisions, the economic effect of which will approximate as closely as possible that of the invalid provisions.

MODIFICATION OF AGREEMENT

27 This Agreement may not be modified or amended except by an instrument in writing duly executed by the parties hereto, and no waiver of compliance with any provision or conditions hereto shall be effective unless evidenced by an instrument in writing, duly executed by the party or parties hereto sought to be charged with such waiver.

GOVERNING LAW

28 This Agreement and the licences granted hereunder shall be governed and construed under and in accordance with the laws of [England]/[the State of _____, United States of America].

SETTLEMENT OF DISPUTES

29 Any controversy or claim arising out of or relating to this agreement or the breach, termination or validity thereof, which cannot be settled amicably by the parties, shall be submitted to arbitration in accordance with the [Commercial Arbitration Rules of the American Arbitration Association] before a panel of three arbitrators. Each party shall appoint one arbitrator and the two arbitrators so appointed shall appoint the third. The venue of the arbitration proceedings shall be [New York, New York]. The arbitration proceedings and all pleadings and correspondence relating thereto shall be in the English language. The decision of the arbitration panel shall be final and binding on the parties and judgment on the award rendered by the arbitrators may be entered in any court having appropriate jurisdiction.

ENTIRE AGREEMENT

30 The terms and conditions herein contained constitute the entire agreement between the parties relating to the subject-matter hereof, and supersede previous communications, whether oral or written, between the parties hereto with respect to the subject-matter hereof, and no previous

agreement or understanding varying or extending the same
shall be binding upon either party thereto.

NOTICES

31   Any notice required or permitted by this Agreement shall
be in writing and shall be sent by registered air mail, or by
confirmed fax, to the parties at the following addresses:

LICENSOR:

....

LICENSEE:

....
....

or to such other address or addresses as the party shall specify
in writing.

IN WITNESS WHEREOF, Licensor and Licensee have caused
their corporate names to be affixed by their duly authorized
officers, effective the day and year first above written.

LICENSOR

By: ....
Title: ....

Attest:

....

LICENSEE

By: ....
Title: ....

Attest:

....

EXHIBIT A
LICENSED PATENTS AND TRADE MARKS

Appendix 5: Typical confidentiality and non-disclosure agreement

---

THIS AGREEMENT is made this _____ day of _____
BETWEEN: _____

AND _____

WHEREAS the parties desire to disclose, each to the other, proprietary and/or confidential information as hereinafter defined for the purpose of evaluating proprietary technology and commercial know-how.

NOW IT IS HEREBY AGREED AS FOLLOWS:

(a) for the purposes of this Agreement 'Proprietary and Confidential Information' shall mean all patent applications, other intellectual property rights, all data, drawings, films, documentation, prototypes, engineering components and machinery and other related commercial, business and financial information of all kinds and in whatsoever form disclosed by one party, the 'Disclosing Party' to the other party, the 'Receiving Party'.

(b) all information so disclosed by the Disclosing Party in written form which is marked as 'Confidential' at the time that it is delivered to the Receiving Party, and all information disclosed by the Disclosing Party to the Receiving

Party orally which is identified to the Receiving Party as being the confidential or proprietary property of the Disclosing Party in a written memorandum delivered to the Receiving Party within fifteen (15) days after the date of the oral disclosure, shall be subject to the terms of this Agreement.

(c)   the Receiving Party shall
  i   hold the Proprietary and Confidential Information confidential to itself, and
  ii   not use the Proprietary and Confidential Information disclosed to it under this Agreement for any purpose other than that referred to above
  iii not disclose Proprietary and Confidential Information disclosed to it under this Agreement to any third party without the Disclosing Party's prior consent in writing thereto.

The obligations and restrictions provided in this clause (c) shall survive termination of this Agreement during such time as the information has not passed into the public domain.

(d)   The obligations and restrictions provided in clause (c) shall not apply to information which is
  i   now or becomes available to the public otherwise than by breach of this Agreement by the Receiving Party, or
  ii   in the restricted possession of the Receiving Party prior to receipt from the Disclosing Party, or
  iii lawfully disclosed to the Receiving Party by a third party without restriction as to use and disclosure.

(e)   The parties hereto understand and agree that the Receiving Party does not acquire by implication or otherwise any right or title to or licence in respect of the Proprietary and Confidential Information.

(f)   On termination of this Agreement for any reason the Receiving Party will return to the Disclosing Party all documents and materials relating to the Proprietary and Confidential Information which it has in its possession.

(g) If during the course of this Agreement the Receiving Party makes any invention or improvement as a result of the Proprietary and Confidential Information disclosed hereunder, the Receiving Party shall have no right or title to or licence in respect of such invention or improvement but will immediately notify the Disclosing Party.

This Agreement is subject to the laws of England.

Signed ....   Signed ....

Name ....   Name ....

Business Title ....   Business Title ....

Appendix 6:
Contents of a bill of lading

1 Consignor
2 Consigned to order of
3 Place of receipt
4 Ocean vessel
5 Port of loading
6 Port of discharge
7 Place of delivery
8 Marks and numbers:
   Number and kind of packages:
   Description of goods:
   Gross weight:
   Measurement
9 Declaration of the interest of consignor
10 Declared value for ad valorem rate
11 Freight amount: Freight payable: Cargo insurance
12 Place and date of issue
13 Stamp and signature

Appendix 7:
Contents of a confirmed irrevocable documentary credit

1   Name of issuing bank
2   Place and date of issue
3   Applicant
4   Advising/confirming bank
5   Partial shipments/transhipment – allowed/not allowed
6   Insurance
7   Shipment from _____: for transportation to _____: not later than _____
8   Expiry date and presentation of document _____
9   Beneficiary
10 Amount
11 Type of credit with nominated bank
      payment at sight
      deferred payment at
      acceptance of drafts at
      negotiation
      against documents attached
12 Advice for the beneficiary
      commercial invoice
      multimodal transport document
      insurance certificate
      certificate of origin of goods

13   Packing list
14   Signature of issuing bank

Appendix 8:
Commodity index

Commodity groups for product identification when importing into the USA
Alcoholic beverage
Animal feeds
Animal pharmaceuticals
Antiques
Apparel, wearing
Appliances, household
Art
Beverages (non-alcoholic)
Bicycles
Biological drugs, materials
Boats and boat equipment
Books, magazines, newspapers and periodicals
Brass
Brushes
Canned foods
Carpets, rugs and textile floor coverings
Ceramics
Chemical substances
China, porcelain, and ceramic tableware and cookware
Cocoa products
Computer hardware
Confectionery (candy)

Cork
Cosmetics
Cotton, raw and woven
Cultural property and artefacts
Currency, coins and negotiable instruments
Cutlery
Dairy products
Drugs for human use
Edible oils
Electronic devices
Engines
Eyeglasses, eyeglass frames, lenses and sunglasses
Firearms and ammunition
Fishery products, seafoods
Flammable products (household)
Flowers, artificial
Flowers, cut
Foods
Footwear
Fruits, vegetables and nuts
Fur and fur products
Furniture
Games (other than video or computer)
Gems and gemstones
Glass and glass products
Hair products
Handcrafts
Hardware
Helmets
Herbs and spices
Homeopathic medicines
Jewellery
Leather goods
Leather hides
Lightbulbs
Lighting, light fixtures
Luggage
Machine tools

Margarine, mayonnaise and salad dressings
Meat and meat products
Media, recorded and unrecorded
Medical devices
Metals, base
Metals, precious
Microchips
Mineral fuels
Minerals and mineral products
Motor vehicles and motor vehicle equipment
Motors
Musical instruments
Optics
Paper and paper products
Paper pulp
Pearls
Perfume
Pesticides and insecticides
Petroleum and petroleum products
Photographic supplies
Plants and plant products
Plastics and plastic products
Poultry, poultry products and eggs
Radiation-producing products
Radio-frequency devices
Radioactive materials and nuclear reactors
Rubber and rubber products
Saddlery
Seeds
Sporting goods
Stereo equipment
Stone and stone products
Sugars, syrups and molasses
Tea and other brewed beverages
Telecommunications equipment
Textile and textile products
Tiles, ceramic
Timber

Tyres
Tobacco products: cigarettes, cigars, etc
Tobacco, raw and semi-cured
Tools
Toys
Umbrellas
Wallpaper
Watches and clocks
Wigs and hairpieces
Wood products
Wool and wool products

Appendix 9:
Index of UK and US organizations, and US customs broker associations

UK organizations

Export development
Association of British Chambers of Commerce
4 Westwood House
Westwood Business Park
Coventry CU4 8HS
Tel: 01203 694484
Fax: 01203 694696

British Chambers of Commerce
9 Tufton Street
London SW1P 3QB
Tel: 0171–222 1555
Fax: 0171–799 2202

British Exporters Associations
16 Dartmouth Street
London SW1H 9BL
Tel: 0171–222 5419
Fax: 0171–799 2468

British Importers Association
Castle House
25 Castlereagh Street
London W1H 5YR
Tel: 0171–724 5900
Fax: 0171–724 5055

British Standards Institution (BSI)
389 Chiswick High Road
London W4 4AL
Tel: 0181–996 7111
Fax: 0181–996 7048

Business Link
33 Queen Street
London EC4 1AP
Tel: 0800 997998
Fax: 0171–653 3901

Central Office of Information (COI)
Hercules House
Hercules Road
London SE1 7DV
Tel: 0171–928 2345
Fax: 0171–928 5037

Chartered Institute of Marketing
Moor Hall
Cookham
Maidenhead
Berks SL6 9QH
Tel: 01628 427500
Fax: 01628 427499

Confederation of British Industry (CBI)
Centre Point
103 New Oxford Street
London WC1A 1DU
Tel: 0171–379 7400
Fax: 0171–240 1578

Department of Trade and Industry
Kingsgate House
66–74 Victoria Street
London SW1E 6SW
Tel: 0171–215 5444
Fax: 0171–215 4231

Department of Trade
Export Licensing Control
66–74 Victoria Street
London SW1E 6SW
Tel: 0171–215 8070
Fax: 0171–215 8564

Export Credits Guarantee Department (ECGD)
2 Exchange Tower
PO Box 2200
Harbour Exchange
London E14 9GS
Tel: 0171–512 7000
Fax: 0171–512 7649

Freight Transport Association Ltd
Hermes House
St Johns Road
Tunbridge Wells
Kent TN4 9VZ
Tel: 01892 526171
Fax: 01892 534989

HM Customs and Excise
Dorset House
Stamford Street
London SE1 9PY
Tel: 0171–202 4227
Fax: 0171–202 4131

Institute of Chartered Shipbrokers
3 St Helens Place
London EC3A 6EJ
Tel: 0171–628 5559
Fax: 0171–628 5445

Institute of Export
64 Clifton Street
London EC2A 4HB
Tel: 0171–247 9812
Fax: 0171–377 5343

Institute of Freight Forwarders Ltd
Redfern House
Browells Lane
Feltham
Middlesex
Tel: 0181–844 2266
Fax: 0181–890 5546

Institute of Packaging
Sysonby Lodge
Nottingham Road
Melton Mowbray
Leics LE13 0NU
Tel: 01664 500055
Fax: 01664 64164

Institute of Practitioners in Advertising
44 Belgrave Square
London SW1X 8QS
Tel: 0171–235 7020
Fax: 0171–245 9904

International Chamber of Commerce (ICC United Kingdom)
British Affiliate ICC
14 Belgrave Square
London SW1X 8PS
Tel: 0171–823 2811
Fax: 0171–235 5447

Department of Trade and Industry
Department of Trade and Industry
Exports to North America Branch
Kingsgate House
66–74 Victoria Street
London SW1E 6SW
Tel: 0171–215 5000 (Main Switchboard)
Tel: 0171–215 4605 (Cross Sectoral)
Tel: 0171–215 4563 (Capital Goods)
Tel: 0171–215 4593 (Consumer Goods)
Fax: 0171–215 4604/8260

Department of Trade and Industry
North American Trade Policy Unit
Kingsgate House
66–74 Victoria Street
London SW1E 6SW
Tel: 0171–215 4447
Fax: 0171–215 5014

DTI Export Licensing Branch and Export Control Organization
Kingsgate House
66–74 Victoria Street
London SW1E 6SW
Tel: 0171–215 8070
Fax: 0171–215 8564

DTI Export Publications
Admail 528
London SW1W 8YT
Tel: 0171–510–0171
Fax: 0171–510 0197

DTI Overseas Promotions Support
Bridge Place
88–89 Eccleston Square
London SW1V 1PT
Tel: 0171–215 5000
Fax: 0171–215 0689/0693

DTI–Export Promoter Policy Unit
Joint Export Promotion Directorate
Kingsgate House
66–74 Victoria Street
London SW1E 6SW
Tel: 0171–215 4528
Fax: 0171–215 8157

Export Market Information Centre
Kingsgate House
66–74 Victoria Street
London SW1E 6SW
Tel: 0171–215 5444
Fax: 0171–215 4231

Information Society Initiative
151 Buckingham Palace Road
London SW1W 9SS
Tel: 0171–215 1294
Fax: 0171–215 1751

The Patent Office
Concept House
Cardiff Road
Newport NP9 1RH
Tel: 01633 814000
Fax: 01633 814444

Other references
American Embassy
24–31 Grosvenor Square
London W1A 1AE
Tel: 0171–499 9000
Fax: 0171–491 4022

British Exporters Association
16 Dartmouth Street
London SW1H 9BL
Tel: 0171–222 5419
Fax: 0171–799 2468

British Franchise Association
Franchise Chambers
Thames View
Newton Road
Henley-on-Thames
Oxon RG9 1HG
Tel: 01491 578049/578050
Fax: 01491 573517

British Marketing Research Society
15 Northburgh Street
London EC1V 0AH
Tel: 0171–490 4911
Fax: 0171–490 0608

Chartered Institute of Marketing
Moor Hall
Cookham
Maidenhead SL6 9QH
Tel: 01628 427500
Fax: 01628 427499

Confederation of British Industry
Centre Point
103 New Oxford Street
London WC1A 1OU
Tel: 0171–379 7400
Fax: 0171–240 1578

Export Intelligence
Prelink Ltd
Export House
87A Wembley Hill Road
Wembley, Middx HA9 8BU
Tel: 0181–900 1313
Fax: 0181–900 1268

Export Credit Guarantee Department
2 Exchange Tower
PO Box 2200
Harbour Exchange Square
London E14 9GS
Tel: 0171–512 7000
Fax: 0171–512 7649

International Marketing Partnership
Abbey House
4 Abbey Orchard Street
London SW1P 2SS
Tel: 0171–233 0310
Fax: 0171–233 0410

SITPRO (Simpler Trade Procedure Board)
151 Buckingham Palace Road
London SW1W 9SS
Tel: 0171–215 0825
Fax: 0171–215 0824

Technical Help to Exporters
BSI Standards
389 Chiswick High Road
London W4 4AL
Tel: 0181–996 7111
Fax: 0181–996 7048

Trinity Business Development
Horsted Keynes Business Park
Haywards Heath
West Sussex RH17 7BA
Tel: 01342 810810
Fax: 01342 811180

US organizations

British commercial services in the United States
British Consulate-General
Marquis One Tower
Suite 2700
245 Peachtree Center Avenue
Atlanta, GA
Tel: (1) 404 524 8823
Fax: (1) 404 524 3153

British Consulate-General
Federal Reserve Plaza
25th Floor
600 Atlantic Avenue
Boston, MA 02210
Tel: (1) 617 248 9555
Fax: (1) 617 248 9578

British Consulate-General
The Wrigley Building
400 North Michigan Avenue
Suite 1300
Chicago, IL 6061
Tel: (1) 312 346 1810
Fax: (1) 312 464 0661

British Consulate
55 Public Square
Suite 1650
Cleveland, OH 44113–1963
Tel: (1) 216 621 7675
Fax: (1) 216 621 2615

British Consulate
813 Stemmons Tower West
2730 Stemmons Freeway
Dallas, TX 75207
Tel: (1) 214 637 3600
Fax: (1) 214 634 9408

British Consulate-General
1100 Milam Building
Suite 2260
1100 Milam
Houston, TX 77002–5506
Tel: (1) 713 659 6275
Fax: (1) 713 659 7094

British Consulate-General
11766 Wilshire Boulevard
Suite 400
Los Angeles, CA 90025
Tel: (1) 310 477 3322
Fax: (1) 310 575 1450

British Consulate
Brickell Bay Office Tower
Suite 2110
1001 South Bayshore Drive
Miami, FL 33131
Tel: (1) 305 374 1522
Fax: (1) 305 374 8196

British Consulate-General
British Trade Office
845 Third Avenue
New York, NY 10022
Tel: (1) 212 745 0495
Fax: (1) 212 745 0456

British Consulate-General
1 Sansome Street
Suite 850
San Francisco, CA 94104
Tel: (1) 415 981 3030
Fax: (1) 415 434 2018

British Consulate
820 First Interstate Center
999 Third Avenue
Seattle, WA 98104
Tel: (1) 206 622 9255
Fax: (1) 206 622 4728

British Embassy
Trade Promotion Section
3100 Massachusetts Avenue, NW
Washington, DC 20008
Tel: (1) 202 462 1340
Fax: (1) 202 789 6265

Other references
Access America Information Services
PO Drawer R
Acworth
Georgia, 30101
Tel: (1) 404 892 1008
Fax: (1) 404 974 1296

American Arbitration Association
140 West 51st Street
New York, NY 10020
Tel: (1) 212 484 4000
Fax: (1) 212 765 4874

The American Association of Advertising Agencies
666 Third Avenue
New York, NY 10017
Tel: (1) 212 682 2500
Fax: (1) 212 682 8136

American Federation of Small Businesses
500 West Madison Street
Suite 1250
Chicago, IL 60605
Tel: (1) 312 353 4528
Fax: (1) 312 886 5688

American National Standards Institute
11 West Forty-second Street
New York, NY 10036
Tel: (1) 212 642 4900
Fax: (1) 212 398 0023

The American Telemarketing Association
5000 Van Nuys Boulevard
Sherman Oaks, CA 91403
Tel: (1) 818 995 7338
Fax: (1) 818 995 0875

The British–American Chamber of Commerce
52 Vanderbilt Avenue
20th Floor
New York, NY 10017
Tel: (1) 212 661 4060
Fax: (1) 212 661 4074

Direct Marketing Association
1120 Avenue of the Americas
New York, NY 10036
Tel: (1) 212 768 7277
Fax: (1) 212 302 6729

International Franchise Association
Suite 900
1350 New York Avenue, NW
Washington, DC 20005
Tel: (1) 202 628 8000
Fax: (1) 202 628 0812

International Trade Association
c/o The Mellinger Company
25620 Rye Canyon Road, Unit B
Valencia, CA 91355
Tel: (1) 805 257 2700
Fax: (1) 805 257 4840

Library of Congress
Independence Avenue SE
Washington, DC 20540
Tel: (1) 202 707 5000
Fax: (1) 202 707 5844

Mead Data Central Inc./Lexis
PO Box 933
Dayton, OH 45401
Tel: (1) 937 865 6800
Fax: (1) 937 865 1211

National Association of Exporting Companies
PO Box 1330
Murray Hill Station
New York, NY 10156
Tel: (1) 212 725 3311
Fax: (1) 212 725 3312

Small Business Administration
409 Third Street SW
Washington, DC 20416
Tel: (1) 202 205 6600
Fax: (1) 202 205 6064

Standard & Poor's Rating Services
A Division of the McGraw-Hill
Companies Inc.
25 Broadway
New York, NY 10004
Tel: (1) 212 208 8000
Fax: (1) 212 208 0077

US Council for International Business
1212 Avenue of the Americas, 21st Floor
New York, NY 10036
Tel: (1) 212 354 4480
Fax: (1) 212 575 0327

US Department of Commerce
Economic Development Administration
14th Street and Constitution Avenue, NW
Washington, DC 20230
Tel: (1) 202 482 5112
Fax: (1) 202 501 4828

US General Services Administration
18th & F Street, NW
Washington, DC 20405–0001
Tel: (1) 202 501 0450
Fax: (1) 202 208 7607

US International Trade Commission
500 East Street, S.W.
Washington, DC 20436
Tel: (1) 202 205 2000
Fax: (1) 202 205 2104

US Federal Trade Commission
Pennsylvania Ave. and 6th Street, NW
Washington, DC 20580
Tel: (1) 202 326 2222
Fax: (1) 202 326 2050

US Patent and Trade Mark Office
Commissioner of Patent and Trade Marks
Washington, DC 20231
Tel: (1) 800 786 9199
Fax: (1) 703 305 7786

US customs broker associations

The National Association
National Customs Broker and Forwarders Association
1 World Trade Center
Suite 1153
New York City, NY 10048
Tel: (1) 212 432 0050
Fax: (1) 212 432 5709

Atlanta
Independent Freight Forwarders and Customs House Brokers
Association of Atlanta
4742-B Aviation Parkway
Atlanta, GA 30349
Tel: (1) 404 761 6785
Fax: (1) 404 669 0226

Baltimore
Baltimore Customhouse Brokers and Forwarders Association
PO Box 2036
The World Trade Center
Baltimore, MD 21203
Tel: (1) 410 539 0540
Fax: (1) 410 547 0935

Boston
Boston Customs Brokers and International Forwarders
Association
160 Second Street
Suite 210
Chelsea, MA 02129
Tel: (1) 617 884 0229
Fax: (1) 617 889 6890

Brownsville
Brownsville Customs Brokers Association
4694 Coffee Port Road
Brownsville, TX 78522–0484
Tel: (1) 512 831 2000
Fax: (1) 512 831 4140

Charleston
Customs Brokers and Freight Forwarders Association of
Charleston, SC, Inc.
185 E. Bay Street
Suite 204
Charleston, SC 29402
Tel: (1) 803 722 8574
Fax: (1) 803 723 7967

Charlotte
Independent Freight Forwarders and Customhouse Brokers
Association of Charlotte, NC, Inc.
PO Box 19308
Charlotte, NC 28219–0308
Tel: (1) 704 357 8511
Fax: (1) 704 357 8515

Chicago
Customs Brokers and Freight Forwarders Association of
Chicago Inc.
9865 W. Leland
Schiller Park, IL 60176
Tel: (1) 708 678 5100
Fax: (1) 708 671 9077

Columbia River
Columbia River Customs Brokers and Forwarders Association
PO Box 20271
Portland, OR 97220
Tel: (1) 503 255 6560
Fax: (1) 503 255 3418

Connecticut
Connecticut Customs Brokers Association
PO Box 268
Old County Road
Windsor Locks, CT 06096
Tel: (1) 203 623 3344
Fax: (1) 203 627 6635

Detroit
Detroit Customhouse Brokers and Foreign Freight Forwarders
Association Inc.
24100 Southfield
Suite 335
Southfield, MI 48075
Tel: (1) 810 557 5100
Fax: (1) 810 557 5113

El Paso
El Paso Customs Brokers Association
9630 Plaza Circle
El Paso, TX 79927
Tel: (1) 915 858 1022
Fax: (1) 915 859 3521

Florida
Florida Customs Brokers and Forwarders Association Inc.
5600 NW 36th Street, Suite 611
Miami, Springs, FL 33166
Tel: (1) 305 871 7177
Fax: (1) 305 871 2712
Mailing address:
PO Box 52–2022
Miami, FL 33152

Hidalgo
Port of Hidalgo Customs Broker Association
1301 High Lowe Drive
Hidalgo, TX 78557
Tel: (1) 210 843 2711
Fax: (1) 210 843 8838

Houston
Houston Customshouse Brokers and Freight Forwarders
Association
PO Box 60044, AMF
Houston, TX 77205
Tel: (1) 713 821 2011
Fax: (1) 713 678 4839

JFK Airport
JFK Airport Customs Brokers Association Inc.
158–12 Rockaway Blvd.
Jamaica, NY 11434
Tel: (1) 718 528 4117
Fax: (1) 718 949 1286

Mobile
Association of Forwarding Agents and Foreign Freight Brokers
of Mobile Inc.
PO Box 403
Mobile, AL 36601
Tel: (1) 334 432 9741
Fax: (1) 334 432 2029

New York
New York Foreign Freight Forwarders and Brokers Association
1 World Trade Center
Suite 1973
New York, NY 10048
Tel: (1) 212 432 1250
Fax: (1) 212 432 5285

Northern Border Association
W.Y. Moberly Inc.
Associated Customs Brokers
PO Box 164
Sweetgrass, MT 59484
Tel: (1) 406 335 2211
Fax: (1) 406 335 2630

North Texas
North Texas Customs Brokers and Foreign Freight Forwarders
Association
1245 Royal Lane
DFW Airport
Dallas, TX 75261
Tel: (1) 214 456 4388
Fax: (1) 214 456 4228

Philadelphia
Philadelphia Customs Brokers and Forwarders Association
PO Box 9074
Essington, PA 19113
Tel: (1) 215 364 3307
Fax: (1) 215 365 0390

San Diego
San Diego District Brokers Association
9051 Siempre Viva Road
Suite J
San Diego, CA 92173
Tel: (1) 619 661 6464
Fax: (1) 619 661 6491

San Francisco
San Francisco Customs Brokers and Freight Forwarders
Association
Fritz Companies, Inc.
706 Mission Street, 10th Floor
San Francisco, CA 94103
Tel: (1) 415 541 8334
Fax: (1) 415 904 8661

Savannah
Independent Freight Forwarders and Customs Brokers Associ-
ation of Savannah Inc.
PO Box 9239
Savannah, GA 81412
Tel: (1) 912 234 7241
Fax: (1) 912 236 5230

Southern Border
Southern Border Customhouse Brokers Association
PO Box 698
Nogales, AZ 85628–0698
Tel: (1) 602 761 6400
Fax: (1) 602 761 6423

Utah
Utah Customs Brokers and Freight Forwarders Association
PO Box 26221
Salt Lake City, UT 84126
Tel: (1) 801 264 9130
Fax: (1) 801 975 7838

Virginia
Customs Brokers and International Freight Forwarders Association of VA
16 Koger Court
Suite 100
Norfolk, VA 23502
Tel: (1) 804 466 1170
Fax: (1) 804 466 1823

Washington State
Customhouse Brokers and International Freight Forwarders Association of Washington State
PO Box L
Blaine, WA 98230
Tel: (1) 206 332 5951
Fax: (1) 206 332 8285

Washington, DC
Washington Custom Brokers and Freight Forwarders Association
Dulles International Airport
Washington, DC 20041
Tel: (1) 703 471 9824
Fax: (1) 703 742 8371

Wilmington
Customs Brokers and Freight Forwarders Association of Wilmington, NC
Wilmington, NC 28402
Tel: (1) 919 763 8491
Fax: (1) 919 763 0445

Wisconsin
Wisconsin Customs Brokers and Forwarders Association
7071 S. 13th Street
Oak Creek, WI 53154
Tel: (1) 414 768 0123
Fax: (1) 414 768 9120

Appendix 10: Glossary

AAA	American Arbitration Association
ADR	Alternative Dispute Resolution
Advising bank	Bank which advises issuing bank that documents required under the letter of credit are in order
All risks	Insurance which has extensive cover but with certain exclusions
AWB	Air Waybill
Back-to-back credit	New credit opened on the basis of an existing non-transferable credit in favour of a different beneficiary
Bill of exchange	Legal document which instructs payment or makes promise to pay
Bill of lading (B/L)	Legal document which confirms title to the goods
'Blue Sky' laws	Exchange security laws of US states
Bonded warehouse	Accommodation for dutiable cargoes which are under customs surveillance
CB	Container base

CFR	Cost and freight. Price of goods includes all costs of shipment and freight to destination
CERCLA	Comprehensive Environment Response Compensation and Liability Act
CIF	Cost, insurance and freight. Price of goods includes all costs of shipment, freight and insurance to destination port
CIFCI	Cost, insurance, freight, commission, interest
COD	Cash on delivery
Confirming bank	Bank requested by issuing bank to confirm that documents required under the letter of credit are in order
CRA	Civil Rights Act
Demurrage	Extra charge made if the loading or unloading is delayed
Documentary credit D/C	Agreement of a bank to pay the buyer on behalf of the seller when specified conditions have been fulfilled
Documentary draft	Bill of exchange drawn by the seller against the buyer and accompanied by shipping documents
Draw-down	The time when funds are paid under a commercial deal
ECGD	Export Credit Guarantee Department
EDGAR	Electronic and Date Gathering Analysis and Retrieval System
EEO	Equal Employment Opportunity
Employment-at-will	Employment relationship terminable at the will of either party

EPA	Environmental Protection Agency
Ex-warehouse	Price of goods including packaging at the warehouse gate
Ex-works	Price of goods including packaging at the works (factory) gate
FAS	Free alongside ship
FCA	Free carrier. Similar to FOB but applies to air, road, rail and roll-on/roll-off ocean shipment
FIO	Free in and out
FOA	Free on board aircraft. Price includes transport to aircraft and loading costs
FOB	Free on board. Price includes transport to ship and loading costs
FOR	Free on rail. Price includes transport to rail truck and loading costs
FOT	Free on truck
FTA	Free Trade Agreement
FTC	Federal Trade Commission
GATT	General Agreement on Tariffs and Trade
GDP	Gross domestic product
ICC	International Chamber of Commerce
Incoterms	Delivery terms set by the International Chamber of Commerce
Issuing bank	Bank issuing the letter of credit on behalf of its customers, the buyer or applicant
LCIA	London Court of International Arbitration

Letter of credit (L/C) *See* Documentary credit

MANA	Manufacturing Agents National Association
NAFTA	North America Free Trade Agreement
OSHA	Occupational Safety and Health Act
Packing List	Document list setting out the goods in each case
PCT	Patent Co-operation Treaty
Performance bond	Bond that guarantees fulfilment of the contract
Pro forma invoice	Preliminary invoice setting out price quotation but on which payment is not intended
Promissory note	Bill of exchange
RCRA	Resource Conservation and Recovery Act
Red clause	Clause authorizing the bank paying under a letter of credit to make unsecured advance payment to the beneficiary
Revolving credit	Letter of credit which, after use, is automatically reissued for further drawing
SEC	Securities Exchange Commission
UCC	Uniform Commercial Code
UNCITRAL	United Nations Commission on International Trade Law
Weight list	Documentary list setting out the weight of individual parcels

WIPO   World Intellectual Property Organization

WTO   World Trade Organization

Appendix 11:
Important arbitration clauses

Suggested clauses for the settlement of disputes through mediation, the mini-trial, arbitration and litigation.

Mediation
'Any controversy or claim arising out of or relating to this contract, or the breach, termination or validity thereof, which cannot be settled amicably by the parties shall be submitted by the parties in good faith to mediation [to be administered by the American Arbitration Association under its Commercial Mediation Rules] before resorting to arbitration, litigation or other dispute resolution procedure.'

Mini-trial
'Any controversy or claim arising out of or relating to this contract, or the breach, termination or validity thereof, which cannot be settled amicably by the parties shall be submitted to a mini-trial [under the Mini-Trial procedures of the American Arbitration Association].'

Arbitration
'Any controversy or claim arising out of or relating to this agreement or the breach, termination or validity thereof, which cannot be settled amicably by the parties, shall be submitted to arbitration in accordance with the [commercial] Arbitration

Rules of the [American Arbitration Association; International Chamber of Commerce] before a panel of three arbitrators. Each party shall appoint one arbitrator and the two arbitrators so appointed shall appoint the third. The venue of the arbitration proceedings shall be [New York, New York]. The arbitration proceedings and all pleadings and correspondence relating thereto shall be in the English language. The decision of the arbitration panel shall be final and binding on the parties and judgment on the award rendered by the arbitrators may be entered in any court having appropriate jurisdiction.'

Litigation
'The parties submit to the exclusive jurisdiction of the courts of [England], and any and all disputes arising under this Agreement shall be resolved by the courts of [England].'

Appendix 12:
Selected US Publications

American Import/Export Management Magazine
North American Publishing Company
401 Broad Street
Philadelphia, PA 19108
Tel: (1) 215 238 5357
Fax: (1) 215 238 5099

Commerce Business Daily
(Overseas Subscriptions)
Superintendent of Documents
US Government Printing Office
Washington, DC 20402–9317
Tel: (1) 202 512 0132
Fax: (1) 202 512 1355

Croner's Reference Book for World Traders
Croner Publications, Inc.
10951 Sorrento Valley Road
San Diego, CA 92121
Tel: (1) 619 546 1894
Fax: (1) 619 546 1955

Customs Regulations of the United States
Superintendent of Documents
US Government Printing Office
Washington, DC 20402
Tel: (1) 202 514 1800
Fax: (1) 202 512 1355

Custom House Guide
North American Publishing Company
401 North Broad Street
Philadelphia, PA 19108
Tel: (1) 215 238 5357
Fax: (1) 215 238 5099

Customs Law and Administration
American Association of Exporters and Importers
11 West 42nd Street
New York, NY 10036
Tel: (1) 212 944 2230
Fax: (1) 212 382 2606

Directory of United States Importers
Journal of Commerce
2 World Trade Center, 27th Floor
New York, NY 10048
Tel: (1) 212 837 7000
Fax: (1) 212 208 0206

Dun & Bradstreet Inc.
One Diamond Hill Road
Murray Hill, NJ 07974
Tel: (1) 908 665 5000
Fax: (1) 908 665 1409

Dun & Bradstreet Information Services
3 Sylvan Way
Parsippany, NJ 07054
Tel: (1) 201 605 6000
Fax: (1) 201 605 6930

Import Bulletin
Journal of Commerce
2 World Trade Center, 27th Floor
New York, NY 10048
Tel: (1) 212 837 7000
Fax: (1) 212 208 0206

Importers Manual USA
(Hinkelman, Edward)
World Trade Press
1505 5th Avenue
San Rafael, CA 94901
Tel: (1) 415 454 9934
Fax: (1) 415 453 7980

Industrial Market Research Inc.
mailing address:
PO Box 4405
Whittier, CA 90607
Tel: (1) 310 698 4862
Fax: (1) 310 693 2341

International Directory of Importers
Croner Publications Inc.
10951 Sorrento Valley Road
San Diego, CA 92121
Tel: (1) 619 546 1894
Fax: (1) 619 546 1955

Journal of Commerce
Journal of Commerce
2 World Trade Center, 27th Floor
New York, NY 10048
Tel: (1) 212 837 7000
Fax: (1) 212 208 0204

Kompass Directories
Croner Publications Inc.
10951 Sorrento Valley Road
San Diego, CA 92121
Tel: (1) 619 546 1894
Fax: (1) 619 546 1955

Predicasts
Information Access Company Inc.
362 Lakeside Drive
Foster City, CA 94404–1146
Tel: (1) 415 378 5000
Fax: (1) 415 378 5369

The Thomas Register
Thomas International Publishing Co.
Five Penn Plaza
New York, NY 10001
Tel: (1) 212 695 0500
Fax: (1) 212 290 7362

Trade Directories of the World
Croner Publications Inc.
10951 Sorrento Valley Road
San Diego, CA 92121
Tel: (1) 619 546 1894
Fax: (1) 619 546 1955

Trade Shows Worldwide
Gale Research Inc.
835 Penobscot Bldg.
Detroit, MI 48226
Tel: (1) 313 961 2242
Fax: (1) 800 414 5043

US Customs Tariffs and Trade
Bureau of National Affairs Inc.
1231 25th Street, NW
Washington, DC 20037
Tel: (1) 202 452 4200
Fax: (1) 202 452 4610

Available from US Customs
Global Trade Talk Official US Customs Service journal for the international trade community. Published bimonthly.

US Customs International Mail Imports Publication No. 514.

United States Import Requirements Publication No. 517

Import Quotas Publication No. 519.

Drawback: A Duty Refund on Certain Imports Publication No. 525.

TIB: Temporary Importation under Bond Publication No. 527.

807 Guide: Import Requirements on Articles Assembled Abroad from US Components. Publication No. 536.

US Customs and Protection of Intellectual Property Rights Publication No. 549.

Tariff Classification of Prospective Imports Publication No. 550.

Questions and Answers on Customs Bonds Publication No. 590.

Foreign Trade Zones US Customs Procedures and Requirements. Publication No. C:79–2.

Appendix 13: British–American chambers of commerce and business associations

California
British–American Chamber of Commerce, Orange County
PO Box 50905–215
Irvine, CA 92619–0905
Tel: (1) 714 452 9292
Fax: (1) 714 452 9292

British–American Chamber of Commerce
41 Sutter Street, Suite 303
San Francisco, CA 94104
Tel: (1) 415 296 8645
Fax: (1) 415 296 9649

British–American Chamber of Commerce of Los Angeles
1640 Fifth Street, Suite 203
Santa Monica, CA 90401
Tel: (1) 310 394 4977
Fax: (1) 310 374 0839

Colorado
British–American Business Association
1801 Broadway, Suite 810
Denver, CO 80215
Tel: (1) 303 296 4333
Fax: 303 296 2223

Florida
British–American Chamber of Commerce, Miami
2655 LeJeune Road, Suite 500
Coral Gables, FL 33134
Tel: (1) 305 444 6627
Fax: (1) 305 448 7605

British–American Business Council of Tampa Bay
4230 South McDill Avenue, Suite 230
Tampa, FL 33611
Tel: (1) 813 832 4780
Fax: (1) 813 835 7626

British–American Chamber of Commerce of Central Florida Inc.
PO Box 618205
Orlando, FL 32861
Tel: (1) 407 363 4821
Fax: (1) 407 363 7336

British–American Chamber of Commerce
Greater Fort Lauderdale
2550 North Federal Highway
Fort Lauderdale, FL 33305
Tel: (1) 954 537 6070
Fax: (1) 954 537 9530

Georgia
British–American Business Group
1199 Euclid Avenue
Atlanta, GA 30307
Tel: (1) 404 681 2224
Fax: (1) 404 522 0132

Illinois
British–American Chamber of Commerce for the Midwest Inc.
Suite 9–112
The Merchandise Mart
200 World Trade Center Chicago
Chicago, IL 60654
Tel: (1) 312 329 0727
Fax: (1) 312 329 1371

Maryland
British–American Business Association, Chesapeake Inc.
c/o World Trade Center Institute
World Trade Center
Baltimore Suite 232,
Baltimore, MD 21202
Tel: (1) 410 576 0022
Fax: (1) 410 576 0751

New England
British–American Business Council of New England Inc.
523 Lewis Wharf
Boston, MA 02110
Tel: (1) 617 720 3622
Fax: (1) 617 720 4331

New York
British–American Chamber of Commerce
52 Vanderbilt Avenue, 20th Floor
New York, NY 10017
Tel: (1) 212 661 4060
Fax: (1) 212 661 4074

North Carolina
British–American Business Council of the Carolinas
100 North Tyron Street, Suite B-200–130
Charlotte, NC 28202
Tel: (1) 704 334 7501
Fax: (1) 704 334 0371

Ohio
British–American Chamber of Commerce, Great Lakes Region
c/o Silk & Co.
530 Leader Building, Superior Avenue
Cleveland, OH 44114
Tel: (1) 216 621 2323
Fax: (1) 216 621 5955

Pennsylvania
British–American Chamber of Commerce, Greater Philadelphia
1234 Market Street, Suite 1800
Philadelphia, PA 19107
Tel: (1) 215 972 3986
Fax: 215 972 3905

British–American Business Council of Pittsburgh Inc.
445 Fort Pitt Blvd.
Suite 220
Pittsburgh, PA 15219
Tel: (1) 412 281 6926
Fax: (1) 412 281 9946

Tennessee
British–American Business Association of Tennessee Inc.
PO Box 50135
Nashville, TN 37205
Tel: (1) 615 259 1033
Fax: (1) 615 259 1030

Texas
British–American Commerce Association
PO Box 225628
Dallas, TX 75222
Tel: (1) 214 941 7356
Fax: (1) 214 941 3103

British–American Business Association
25211 Grogan's Mill Road
The Woodlands, TX 77380
Tel: (1) 713 367 7796
Fax: (1) 713 292 4234

Washington
British–American Business Council of the Pacific Northwest
3100 Two Union Square
601 Union Street
Seattle, WA 98101
Tel: (1) 206 622 9255 ext. 4427
Fax: (1) 206 292 4233

Washington, DC
British–American Business Association of Washington, D.C., Inc.
PO Box 17482
Washington, DC 20041
Tel: (1) 202 293 0010
Fax: (1) 202 296 3332

United Kingdom
The British–American Chamber of Commerce
8 Staple Inn
London WC1V 7QH
Tel: 0171–404 6400
Fax: 0171 404 6828

British-American Business Council of the West of England
The Old Vicarage
Somerset Square, Nailsea
Bristol BS19 2DW
Tel: 01275 856700
Fax: 01275 858569

British–American Business Group in the North West
Alexandra House
Borough Road
St Helens
Merseyside WA10 3TN
Tel: 01744 451060
Fax: 01744 453377

Associate members

Canada
British–American Business Association (Associate member)
7100 Woodbine Ave., Unit 305
Markham, Ontario, L3R 5J2
Tel: (1) 905 475 3896
Fax: (1) 905 475 0311

Mexico
British–Mexican Chamber of Commerce (Associate Member)
Camara de Comercio Britanica, AC
Rio de la Plata, No 30
Col. Cuahtemoc Mexico, DF 06500
Tel: (52) 5 2560901
Fax: (52) 5 2115451

Index

Unless otherwise stated references are to the location and institutions in the United States

The Business Plan - Approved!

G Nigel Cohen

The Business Plan - Approved! is a comprehensive guide to creating an impressive and achievable business plan to win the approval of your bank manager and investors. It will help you to evaluate the business from the viewpoints of sales, costs, and cash and assimilate the information into a clearly defined business strategy. Written in a clear, down-to-earth style, with no technical jargon, it encourages you to see your business plan as a potential investor in the company would, answering some basic but crucial questions along the way • What is a business plan and why do we need one? • How do we go about creating a successful business plan? • What do banks and investors look for?

All aspects of the business plan are dealt with, from initial planning in order to decide which direction the business should follow, through to presenting the plan in a professional and persuasive document. Guidance is also provided on how to set the plan out in the style that bankers and investors expect to see.

Written by accountants with many years' experience of getting plans approved and vetting them for banks and investors, uniquely this book also includes the expert opinions of investors and lawyers themselves describing what makes them accept or reject a business plan. Two real life examples are provided as models and to focus the reader on common pitfalls.

The practical, no-nonsense guidance of *The Business Plan - Approved!* will be welcomed by anyone planning to grow a business, start up on their own, or, as a manager, justify their budget for the coming year.

Gower

Clinch That Deal

Harry A Mills

Harry Mills wrote *Negotiate* after deciding that a handbook on negotiation had to have several essential features, and failing to find any that did. These features were: practicality, with tips, techniques and strategies taken from real life; user-friendliness, with checklists of key points; skills-focused, explaining how as well as what; and realistic about what to do when negotiations don't go according to plan.

The result is an accessible book for all negotiating situations. It describes in detail the strategies and skills you need to become a master negotiator. In seven easy steps you will learn how to turn conflict into agreement and win-lose contests into win-win settlements.

Harry Mills draws on his wide experience as a consultant and negotiator to explain:

- The seven easy steps to agreement
- How to choose the best approach
- How to uncover the other side's real needs
- How to trade concessions
- How to build rapport
- How to make time work for you
- How to increase your bargaining power
- How to avoid expensive mistakes
- How to counter negative tactics
- How to build productive relationships
- How to create deals which serve the best interests of both sides.

Gower

The Complete Guide to Quick and Easy Marketing that Works

David N Russell

Need a helping hand with your sales and marketing efforts? Want to know how to generate extra profits quickly, without having to wade through time-consuming theory?

If so, David Russell's book is just what you need. Written in a style that you will enjoy and understand immediately, with summary points and quick tips throughout, it's marketing without the mystique. There's no room for jargon here, its pages are simply packed with ideas and tips which are guaranteed to make any sales and marketing effort more effective immediately. It's designed to put you ahead of your competitors and to keep you ahead.

Hundreds of common sense, no nonsense, practical ideas will help you:

- Make your advertising more effective
- Use public relations effectively
- Write an effective press release
- Write an effective direct mail letter
- Increase response from a direct mail campaign
- Make an exhibition stand really work for you
- Keep your customers
- Find more customers
- Stay one step ahead of the competition

And much, much more.

Gower

How to Make More Profit

Michael K Lawson

What determines the profitability of your business? How can you identify the critical factors and turn them to your advantage? These questions lie at the heart of Michael Lawson's book.

Using a model based on the experience of more than 300 companies he examines the three groups of factors that influence the success of any business: the external environment, the communication process and the business process. These three areas are intimately linked, so that changes in any one of them will affect the others. Practical and down-to-earth throughout, the book shows you how to pinpoint the key profit-related problems - and what to do about them. Whether you are responsible for a complete business or just one unit or function, whether you work in a large company or a small one, *How to Make More Profit* will enable you to do just that.

Gower

How to Negotiate Worldwide

A Practical Handbook

Donald W Hendon and Rebecca Angeles Hendon

As the world continues to shrink, the ability to operate on a global scale is becoming a necessity for more and more business people. And the rewards of knowing how to negotiate in different markets can be enormous.

This book is based on the experience of thousands of managers who have attended the seminars run by the authors in more than twenty countries. From it you will learn: how changing conditions in international business are affecting the way people negotiate; the distinct stages of negotiation; the price concession patterns preferred by executives from fifteen different countries; how to observe, interpret and use non-verbal behaviour across a range of cultures; the seventy-three favourite tactics chosen by executives from eleven countries - and how to counter them. With anecdotes, case studies, exercises, checklists and a cultural self-awareness questionnaire, here is a book that actively involves the reader.

If you are one of the increasing number of managers who expect to deal with, work with, or live among members of different cultures, then this book is for you.

Gower

How to Write Effective Reports

Second Edition

John Sussams

In business, administration and research, the report is an indispensable tool and all managers or specialists need to master the skills involved in writing one. John Sussams' book covers all aspects of the subject in a thoroughly practical fashion. It not only discusses language and style but also explains how to structure and organize material to facilitate understanding. In addition it deals with planning, presentation and production.

The text is enlivened by examples and illustrations and there are a number of exercises designed to improve the reader's report-writing ability.

Gower

How World Class Companies Became World Class

Studies in Corporate Dynamism

Cuno Pümpin

The globalization of the world economy, unpredictable political developments, dramatic changes in international financial markets, new information technology - to name but a few factors have created a turbulent and rapidly changing business environment. Only dynamic companies will be able to survive under these conditions.

In this innovative book, Cuno Pümpin illustrates how many of the world's most successful corporations have used dynamic principles to increase their market share, multiply their turnover, and unlock value for both shareholders and employees. The author's findings are based on analysis of many successful and dynamic American, European and Japanese corporations. During intensive interviews with top managers, a pattern of how these companies reacted to the challenges of a turbulent environment emerged.

This book focuses on how the dynamic principles practised by these companies have led to their common success, during times when many other companies have failed.

Gower

The Management Skills Book

Conor Hannaway and Gabriel Hunt

There is virtually no limit to the skills a manager is expected to use. Some are required every day, others once a month or even once a year. From managing employee performance to chairing meetings, from interviewing staff to making retirement presentations, the list seems endless. How can managers be effective in all these areas? How can they know what to do in every situation?

The Management Skills Book is designed to help all managers facing the challenge of constant change. It is an easy-to-access practical reference work setting out in more than 100 brief guides the elements of the skills needed to succeed as a manager. Each guide is presented in a clear point-by-point style enabling the reader to absorb the key ideas without having to work through a tangle of theory.

New and experienced managers alike will welcome the book as a powerful aid to increased effectiveness.

Gower

Practical Media Relations

Judith Ridgway

This enlarged and updated edition of *Successful Media Relations* describes the basic skills and techniques involved in a way that will be helpful to students and practitioners alike. Judith Ridgway has been both a public relations executive and a journalist and so is ideally equipped to explain their different points of view.

She starts by showing how to construct a realistic programme and how the relevant activities can be planned and assessed in the light of organizational objectives. The book covers not only the standard tools of communication such as press releases, mailing lists, photographs, TV and radio interviews, competitions and special offers, but also events like press conferences, factory visits, new product launches and sponsored radio and TV. A feature of this new edition is the attention paid to electronic communications, including the use of computers, scanners, modems and satellite telephones.

Throughout the text actual examples are given by way of illustration. There are practical hints and tips in abundance and a series of comprehensive checklists. Each chapter ends with a useful summary. As an introduction to the world of modern media relations Judith Ridgway's book would be hard to better.

Gower